hyperwest

american residential architecture

Alan Hess
Photography by Alan Weintraub

n the edge

Whitney Library of Design
an imprint of Watson-Guptill Publications / New York

For Zoë and Nash, my great traveling partners – A. H.

For my father, my mother, Susan, and Cynthia – A. W.

Acknowledgments
The author and photographer would like to thank the owners
of each of these houses for their generosity and helpfulness
in allowing us to see and photograph their homes. Each has
a special appreciation of their remarkable houses. We would
also like to thank the architects who gave their time to help
us with this project; special thanks to Nash, Zoë, and Tiena
as well. – A. H., A. W

HALF-TITLE PAGE Hill house
TITLE PAGE Tabancay house
THIS PAGE Becker house
CONTENTS PAGE (LEFT TO RIGHT) Empie, Tabancay and Sonoma houses

© 1996 Thames and Hudson Ltd, London
Text © Alan Hess
Photographs © Alan Weintraub

First published in the United States by Whitney Library of Design, an imprint
of Watson-Guptill Publications, 1515 Broadway, New York, NY 10036.

Library of Congress Cataloging-in-Publication Data
Hess, Alan.
    Hyperwest : American residential architecture on the edge / by Alan
Hess; photography by Alan Weintraub.
        p.   cm.
    Includes index.
    ISBN 0–8230–2520–9
    1. Architecture, Domestic—West (U.S.) 2. Architecture, Modern—
20th century—West (U.S.) I. Title.
NA7223.H47   1996
728'.372'097809045—dc20   96–22312
                                               CIP

Manufactured in Hong Kong

First printing, 1996

1 2 3 4 5 6 7 8 9/02 01 00 99 98 97 96

Contents

technowest

introduction

T he American West has always been an eccentric place. The landscape is audacious, gaudy and boastful, its people dissatisfied with tradition and eager to reinvent themselves. Until fairly recently it has been a far-away land where the prying eyes of East Coast convention could not peer. The people of the West and the place itself have conspired to push their culture off-center and out to the edge. Nowhere is this seen more plainly than in the highly personal designs Westerners build for their own homes.

A little over a hundred years ago Westerners began to relax from the labors of making a safe shelter for themselves in the wilderness and to reflect on their position in a new world. As they considered their surroundings and their relation to the rest of the world, certain attitudes emerged from three unavoidable facts: the presence of nature, the lack of immediate history and a dependence on technology. Over the years the West's wide open spaces and a spirit of liberation have given builders and architects license to create a cutting-edge architecture exploring these themes. With that license they have attempted to build the unlikely and the impossible: houses

ABOVE RIGHT Sidley house, Malibu, California
BELOW Tsui house, Berkeley, California

that are crystalline caves, cozy bungalows that pretend to
be grand monuments, comfortable habitats in the inhospitable
desert. Today Western architects push the limits as much as
ever, and that is the spirit of Hyperwest architecture. With
the right client and the right site, almost anything can be
designed and built.

At first glance the range of shapes and styles of the
houses in this book might hardly seem to exist in the same
universe, let alone the same region. There are astonishing
organic buildings, live-in seashells that look as if they
might scuttle away; there are witty variations on ancient
ruins, Moorish fantasies and Craftsman delights that
transport us to the long ago and far away; and there
are building-size microchips that push modern materials
to the limit.

ABOVE Fuller house, Carefree,
Arizona
BELOW LEFT Jordan house,
Oakland, California

What these houses have in common
is a willingness to push toward the edge –
an edginess, if you will. In the mythic West,
the place with no past and a future to be
invented, the primary architectural tradition
is grounded in a search for the ever-shifting
frontier. Despite the striking differences

among these residences, there are overlapping ideas: nature is as much a part of the calculations of Edward Niles's steely high-tech houses as technology is in Bart Prince's flowing organic spaces. Such diversity is intrinsic to the Western culture, as is the impulse to merge and combine opposites, but underlying all these designs is a uniquely Western combination of attitudes: the right to be different, cherished memories borne lightly, the impulse to innovate, an inescapable attachment to the natural and human landscapes of the West – the sublime mountains, the wide desert and ocean, the rowdy cities.

Nature, history and machines – these are the raw materials that the West's architects have mined from pioneer days to today. Nature's vast distances, harsh deserts and insurmountable mountains established the cruel ground rules for human habitation, but its

fertile land, awesome vistas and sacred isolation also inspired people
to make the daring move west, to create their own cultural identity.
History is the baggage people brought with them, some of which
was discarded along the trail, some of which was used to fashion
a happier reality than they had in Europe, the East Coast or Asia.
Machines provided the means by which both nature and history
could be reshaped to meet the human imagination.

Paradoxically, this is a book about traditions in a place where
tradition was rejected. Caught up in this conundrum, many of the
books and publications about recent Western architecture
concentrate on immediate trends, on innovations, on the latest styles.
But just because Westerners fled from traditions does not mean they
did not evolve their own. Now, more than a century after the closing
of the frontier, it is time to recognize those traditions.

The houses presented here were constructed over the past two decades and show the state of these traditions today. Organic architecture, for example, was introduced by Frank Lloyd Wright, who was born in Wisconsin shortly after the Civil War, when Chicago was considered to be in the West. The recent houses in the style he pioneered reflect a lively, progressive – though not widely documented – tradition.

ABOVE RIGHT Tabancay house, Oakland, California
BELOW Rainbow house, Julian, California

These houses also pay tribute to popular traditions – not an insignificant attribute in a democratic culture that undermines class distinctions and blurs the line between popular and high art. Culture in the West does not just trickle down from the high-art taste-makers to the masses; architects are just as likely to be inspired by the billboards, the asphalt shingles, the modest bungalows of Western vernacular culture. In the words of the late critic John Beach, "The fusion of the educated and the raw, the sophisticated and the unsophisticated, the high art and the low art ... is the aspect of the work of [Bernard] Maybeck and Willis Polk and Ernest Coxhead" that forms a foundation for the tradition of popular design mixed with high art.

This mix is seen at many levels. Hyperwest houses often embrace the standard materials and construction techniques of building contractors – the vernacular of the building trades. Ace Architects and Kotas/Pantaleoni use off-the-shelf items in ways that would never have been anticipated. Their designs glory in the thin, ephemeral and suggestive quality of these materials, extending their expressive potential by, for example, turning silo caps into Moorish domes and corrugated aluminum into rocket-ship nacelles. Not even Edward Niles's polished steel connections and columns are exotic custom fabrications, but practical standardized systems, common components in commercial offices or shops. In a culture where a machine, in the guise of the family car, becomes a family member, an understanding

ABOVE Sonoma house, Stewarts Point, California
BELOW LEFT Sidley house, Malibu, California

of and affinity for technology is widely and deeply rooted. This is an American style, not refined or elegant but mass market and popular. In the West the most is made of little, and in the process, the usual rules about what constitutes significant architecture are subverted.

Democratic diversity, the West's traditions, the influence of mass culture and freedom: these are the threads that unite Hyperwest architecture. Here we see freedom and individuality not just as clichés but as real qualities for which people strive and sacrifice to build for their lifetimes. Some of the houses are costly and large, some are modest and done on the cheap. Some are penthouses, some vacation homes, some home-offices. Sites range from ocean to desert, from

FROM LEFT Overstreet house, Corte Madera, California; Tabancay house, Oakland, California; Kurlander house, San Francisco, California; Price house, Corona del Mar, California; Sheats-Goldstein house, Beverly Hills, California; Feldman house, Sedona, Arizona

mountain to suburb, from city to wilderness. It doesn't matter.

Proud and eccentric individualism is seen in each of these out-of-the-mainstream buildings, a marginalism that invests ordinary things with meaning and shows how humans view the wild nature they must live with. Historical architecture tells the story of what is important to us in our collective memories. Technology became more than a simple tool long ago. These cutting-edge designs grapple with these issues richly and broadly. If these designs cry out, if they run roughshod over convention, if they refuse to stay within the polite constraints of taste, if they rewrite the rules and contradict each other, so much the better. They are using every means at their disposal to clear the way for the mainstream to follow.

"I like the freedom in West Coast architecture," a well-known high-art architect assured himself several years ago. "But sometimes I think there is too much freedom."

If there is such a thing as too much architectural freedom, the houses in this chapter are ample testimony. Yet there is something instructive about the excess. These houses are what Modern architecture was supposed to be, about freedom and unshackled exuberance – before it was hijacked by the International Style. These buildings smash every conception about what a room, a hallway or a wall should be, and they reinvent the catalogue of elements by drawing on an encyclopedic range of sources. Structures can be nests, insects, flowers. In the hands of experienced and imaginative architects like these, it works.

Historically, most architecture has been based on other architecture – whether on Greek temples or Gothic cathedrals, or modern factories and grain elevators. In the West, however, nature's presence is so pervasive that architects have been forced to look beyond the man-made for inspiration. Nature ultimately controls everything in the American West – cities, lives, the very shape of the landscape. Earthquakes shake apart the mightiest bridges and scramble city plans. A house shrivels into insignificance in the shadow of basin and range. These residences tell the story of how Westerners have embraced nature's challenge.

Whiplashing lines, unconventional biomorphic structures emerging from the soil – the nonconformist superficial features in many organic buildings usually conceal a wide variety of approaches used to arrive at such forms. There is no such thing as a single organic style. Some organic buildings draw on biological sources, with windows taking on the appearance of eyes and façades becoming faces. Rooflines sprout antennae, columns become spindly legs.

Eugene Tsui's Berkeley house re-creates life inside a seashell by using technologically ingenious materials: panels that can be cut into blocks are made of concrete and recycled Styrofoam, while the house's ovaloid shape contributes to its stability in earthquake country. Nature and machine are interwoven. Bart Prince, on the other hand, considers organic architecture a set of relationships: a trunk and a leaf have very different forms and functions, yet both relate to the tree. His houses tear apart the conventional

Buildings that grow out of the landscape – or create a landscape of their own.
CLOCKWISE FROM TOP LEFT
Empie house by Charles F. Johnson, Gradow house by Bart Prince, Tsui house by Eugene Tsui, Rainbow house by James Hubbell.

relationships of living spaces to the outdoors, of corridors to rooms, which are then reconstructed afresh according to logic, program, structure and client. His designs contain solid, sensible structure and gaudy plumage, dramatically contrasting textures and colors, all in a singular organic whole.

Some architects employ meadows, cliffs, streams, forests, hills and caves as models to shape rooms and to blend a house into its *genius loci*, but architects who borrow from nature have a challenge if they are to compete with the original. There is simply no finer architectural form, for example, than the extravagantly weird upheaval of red rock in the Navajo nation of northwest Arizona. There are no skyscrapers more daring than the red sandstone pinnacles at Arches National Monument in Utah.

Charles F. Johnson interprets nature as the landscape and its artifacts. Redefining an outcropping of huge rocks as a human habitat, Johnson has created in the Empie house an experience of boulders, their deep-rooted stability, their massiveness, their weather-worn surfaces. It is shelter at its most elemental: it formalizes the ancient process of throwing a few sticks between rocky supports to create an instant shelter from the baking sun.

Some approaches to organic architecture are experiential investigations into the tactile warmth of wood, the heaviness of rock, the softness of rounded forms. Some designers see nature as a mystical force. James Hubbell, for example, a sculptor who works in the medium of architecture, translates natural shapes and details into abstract sculpture, and dematerializes surfaces with color and pattern.

Most of these architects' devices can be traced back to the tenets of Frank Lloyd Wright, father of contemporary organic architecture. The undoubted genius of Wright's interpretation of nature and the machine has been hailed for almost an entire century, yet his influence is seen precious little today, despite a thriving cottage industry that has reduced Wright's fertile imagination to a catalog of accessories. Though none of these Hyperwest houses could be

called Wrightian, they offer some comfort to the notion that there is more to his legacy today than Wright-patterned earrings and ties. In the hands of these architects, Wright's tradition lives.

John Lautner was one of Wright's first apprentices in the 1930s, but in 1939 he had the courage to leave Taliesin – Wright's western studio in Scottsdale, Arizona – to set out on his own course in organic architecture. Wallace Cunningham also studied at Taliesin, though after Wright's death. Bart Prince, Mickey Muennig, Robert Overstreet and Eugene Tsui all worked or studied with Oklahoma architect Bruce Goff, who was himself an admirer and colleague of Wright. Like Lautner, though, he wisely kept his professional distance from the magnetic pull of Wright's influence. As a result, Goff helped to expand the spectrum of organic architecture. Organic architecture's affirmation of pantinaed color, fluid splendor, unconfined diversity and unbounded imagination are a rebuke to the simplicities of chaste, minimalist architecture. The spaces are emotional and complex, not clarified and reductive. Yet even today these extraordinary structures, the seeming antithesis of all things modern, come closest to retaining the spirit of the early modern revolution when everything seemed possible, when houses could be built of glass and roofs could defy gravity. Imagination unchained is allowed to wander – and then to build.

As a group these residences say something about how Westerners have come to terms with nature. They radiate a mighty optimism, embody a kinship between humans and nature. They all seek to strengthen that relationship by creating a place for humans to live with nature. The drama, awe and danger in the Western landscape have always challenged architects' notions of habitation, but in this wild frontier they revel in the sublime and luxuriant beauty of the geology and biology. Unstraitjacketed by convention or mere taste, they exuberantly embrace the spirit of freedom to create the fullest possible expression of human habitat.

Surrounding their inhabitants with organic shapes and textures, these houses build bridges between the human and natural worlds.
FROM LEFT Whiting and Prince houses by Bart Prince, Rancho California house by Kendrick Kellogg, Empie house by Charles F. Johnson.

Bart Prince

Whiting House, Sun Valley, Idaho

BELOW Seen from a bird's eye, the house appears to grow out of the earth. The rolling landscape hides the split-faced concrete-block base (containing garage and services) that raises the living quarters well above the blanket of winter snow. OPPOSITE The varied curves of the house, akin to a natural formation, make it one with the gentle curves of the central Idaho mountains.

How could a single house sit so confidently in such natural grandeur? The Whiting house (1992) does not compete with the landscape, nor does it try to blend in. In the Idaho plain, in a valley of the Sawtooth Range near the famous Sun Valley ski resort, the house makes the landscape itself come alive. The humpbacked ridges encircling it might well be big sisters to its dragon-like form. Its serpentine spine, rising and twisting, becomes an extension of the landscape. The visual references to serpents are not literal, of course: the living room at the house's center is covered by an arched skylight, with the structure's wood ribs exposed under glass. Separate master bedroom and guest wings are more solid, enclosed forms marked by split-faced concrete walls that rise from the foundation. What is achieved is a unity of human habitation and natural setting.

As the long corridor running the length of the house meanders, the visitor is plunged sequentially into restful darkness and cheerful sunlight, but slowly one becomes aware of the house itself (as well as of the glorious scenery) as windows and ribs, opened up in glass, frame views of the structure against the natural backdrop. The organic design captures the organic site. The building and nature become one, but each retains its individuality – a primary concept in organic architecture. Architects working in the organic tradition keep alive the possibility of new ways of doing architecture, and innovative means to connect humans to their environment.

BELOW The corridor that winds through the house exits the shell at one point and wraps itself around the block exterior on its way to one of the bedroom wings. From the windows the house always has views of itself in relation to the landscape.

ABOVE The roof's snaking spine echoes the shapes of river,
road and mountain ridge. At the peak, the wood frame
opens up to become the skylight over the living room.

RIGHT Built-in sofas and tables blend
with the curving walls of the structure.
After passing through this high light-filled
space, the corridor slopes down and
passes into a darker, more intimate space
on its way to the private bedroom wing.
LEFT The primary corridor spine widens
to create the main living spaces. The
fireplace, faced with concrete block,
anchors a conversation area.
OPPOSITE A view back from the
bedroom wing shows the play of light,
sky and shadow that occurs throughout
the house.

BELOW Native *palo verde* trees and Saguaro cactus
surround the desert floor's massive granite outcroppings.
Natural cracks between boulders are filled with glass
to weatherproof the house.
OPPOSITE The master bedroom rises like a watchtower
above the boulders. Like the indigenous pueblo buildings
of the American Southwest, the residence's flat roofs
are used as terraces. Unlike the traditional architecture,
windows pierce the masonry walls. *Vigas* – the ends
of wood roof-beams – pierce the stucco walls.

Charles F. Johnson
> Empie House, Carefree, Arizona

The walls of this house (1982) had waited for more
than 570 million years for a roof before Charles Johnson
came along. The golden-toned granite boulders that
stretch ninety-five feet are the remains of a Precambrian
mountain, tilting slightly north to create a shelter at
the front door. Rooted deeply and solidly in the desert
sand, these boulders enclose the house within a
primeval serenity.

The great hall occupies the space between two large
outcroppings. The architect roofed the space between
these natural columns with heavy *vigas* – the rough-hewn
log beams common in early southwestern architecture
– inserted into the boulders. In the middle of the room
is a plaster-covered fireplace, massive in size yet supple
in form, whose surfaces the architect sculpted by hand,
a reminder of the southwestern tradition of adobe
stoves and walls.

With the master suite perched at the highest point
amid the boulders, the rest of the house circles around
the south and east side of the outcropping. The inner
wall of each room is a wall of boulders, and the outer
wall is concrete block covered in stucco. One guest
room's fireplace sits under a large shelf of rock – a place
where the owners discovered evidence of a prehistoric
fire pit used by the native people.

On a site that has been inhabited for a long, long
time, this is not just architecture about nature, it is
nature itself.

ABOVE Beams of the 16-foot ceilings rest atop the boulders that make up one wall of the house's great hall. A concrete floor was poured to raise and flatten the natural floor of the desert. The ladder is typical of pueblo architecture.

LEFT Used as a fire pit for hundreds of years, this natural overhang was incorporated into the guest room.

OPPOSITE The uneven plaster surfaces of the great hall's fireplace were virtually hand-sculpted by the architect over a concrete-block core. Beyond it is the dining room (right) and kitchen (left). Zuni and other pots by Native Americans rest on the mantle and over the doorways.

James Hubbell

Boys' House, San Diego County, California

When his sons grew old enough, sculptor James Hubbell built them a house in 1984 as part of a compound in the oak-covered mountains outside San Diego that now includes the family residence, the artist's studio and his workshops. Like all of the buildings Hubbell has designed over the last thirty years, the house is sculpture to be inhabited. Its spaces and walls grow out of an organic sense of form, rendering in solid wall the flowing movements of life. The human body walking through space moves in curves and rhythms, not in straight lines and right angles. The rolling shapes of the roof and spires of this unorthodox home fit gently into the scenery's mountain tops.

Entering the house is like descending into a cave. The interior is made up of three main areas – a loft, a sleeping area, a fireplace room. The dazzling bathroom – a fountain of moving color that sprays up and around the rocklike sink, fixtures and walls like quartz squeezing through fissures of rock – is topped with a stained-glass skylight. The entire bungalow is ornamented with colored glass, ceramic tile and seashells, dripping and sparkling like sunlight creeping over a windowsill in the morning.

ABOVE LEFT Irregular left-over brick, ceramic tiles and abalone shells blend together in an organic continuity of flowing space, form and materials in the bathroom. A stained-glass skylight creates a luminescent sky.
LEFT The concrete shapes were first sculpted in a clay model, then sprayed on over full-scale steel armature. Stained-glass windows were fabricated at Hubbell's shops on site.

Every detail, from walls to stair treads to door hinges,
is hand-crafted. Yet it is the unified vision that makes
this house art. Space and structure flow together – lines
move in harmony, ornamental tile picks up where the
sun's rays, colored by stained glass, leave off. Brick is
from a local factory, but Hubbell chose the discarded,
fragments that would have been unusable in conventional
construction.

ABOVE Beneath this ceiling an ordinary
bathtub would be out of place, but this
custom-made tub curves and arcs with the
rest of the building. The ceramic-tile design
accentuates the lines as they meld into
the plaster wall. Taps and handles are also
custom designs.

OPPOSITE Stone from a mountain site
seems to rise out of the ground to create
the foundation for the house. Thick
eyebrows over the windows and the deep-
set front door echo the massive, sheltering
qualities of natural rock outcroppings. The
owner's daughter loves horses, so Hubbell
sculpted a ceramic horse head that appears
to grow out of the wall.

James Hubbell

Rainbow House, Julian, California

On the mountain ridge dividing the Pacific Ocean
from the inland deserts of California, reddish-tan boulders
crop up among the scrub brush and oak trees. It is easy to
see the similarity between the arcs and irregular domes of
the Rainbow house (1988) and the billowing forms of such
boulders, but it is more than an imitation of nature. It
creates its own realm.

The house was designed by Hubbell using a clay model,
with room for improvisation on site as the owner's family,
the designer and his apprentices built it over a period of
almost ten years. Beneath the house's sprayed-concrete shell,
integrally colored with orange and brown pigments, is a
steel framework.

The lower level contains the living room, kitchen and
a greenhouse to one side. Upstairs the master suite and
a guest room occupy the dome. A patio and breezeway
connect the main house to a one-story bedroom, which was
the site's original buildings. Low stone walls meander out
from the structure into the land like the roots of a tree.

Everywhere, Hubbell takes advantage of moments for
ornament: a gap between a balcony and the house is filled
with a spider-web filigree of metal; a light in the ceiling
above the stairwell is an encrustation of glass shards and
small light bulbs that grow out of the stuccoed surface;
a sea of hexagonal tiles twist and turn on the floor, cascading
down steps, parting to reveal a brilliant ceramic tile phoenix.

BELOW Faceted stained-glass windows shine like crystals in the curvaceous walls. The kitchen windows face the Southern California coastline.

OPPOSITE Wood shingles layered in undulating patterns up to twenty thicknesses deep spread over the sculpted roof and walls.

Bart Prince

Price House, Corona Del Mar, California

Like a Zen garden, the Price house (1984) captures an entire landscape in miniature. Though at first the oceanside house seems impenetrable (the entrance is a wood grotto, walled in waves of shingling), like Aladdin's cave it opens into a hidden realm. The interior evokes forests and caves filled with rainbow colors, surface textures tempting to touch and richly crafted woodwork. The abundance of patterns and forms is startlingly rich, but a glance at the Pacific beyond, with its rocky, ragged border and ever-shifting patterns of tide and reflected sunlight, tells us that this is how nature itself is, too. Bart Prince has simply brought the variety of nature – its forests and oceans, its caves and streams – into this dwelling.

Outside, Prince fashioned an undulating roof that appears like a rock cliff in a delicate Japanese landscape. Or perhaps it's a cloud. The design evokes many things, but it does not imitate any one thing. A concealed door leads to the family quarters and a pool and garden completely hidden from the street. Most of the windows direct the eye to the ocean and the sky, appropriating the warm Southern California coastline as its own.

Astonishing architecture runs in the owner's family. Joe Price's mother asked Cliff May to design a house for them in their native Bartlesville, Oklahoma, in 1947; his father commissioned Frank Lloyd Wright to build the Price Tower there in 1952 and a house in Phoenix in 1956. Joe Price himself asked Bruce Goff to design a now-legendary Bartlesville residence in 1956. The Corona del Mar house continues the family tradition with its astonishing mastery of space.

RIGHT The main entrance is a grotto of wood with a concealed entrance. Stairs to the owner's office are plastic outcroppings set in steel treads.
BELOW The view from the second-level study opens to the ocean with views of the rocky coastline.

ABOVE The U-shaped house wraps around a south-facing pool courtyard. The pool is terraced like a tide pool, with black marble steps from the deck area leading down into the water. A round window embellished with shingles and spoke mullions looks into the private family wing.

LEFT Three of these imaginative tree-like constructions function as the house's main structure. The trunk is a two-story bundle of laminated-wood columns, fastened to steel gussets on a concrete foundation. Overhead they splay out like branches, before draping down and curving back in to rejoin the trunk. The spiral stair leads up to the study.

Robert Overstreet

Overstreet House, Corte Madera, California

Sitting on the north side of a wooded hill overlooking San Francisco Bay, this is a house whose interior is filled with degrees of shade and light, creating a sensation much like that of the nearby redwood groves of California's north coast. Light boxes capture the sun and filter light down through three levels. The house rests lightly on the hill: only the stilts (tree trunks stripped of their bark), constitute the structural frame; they root the residence in the earth. As one wanders through the house, the poles add further reminders of the forest. Walkways and gazebos are lifted into the air, looking down on the lushly landscaped hillside.

Some of the boxes filling in the frame are glass-sided; some are solid, covered in plywood. Some are ornamental, with jewel-like windows. The interlocking, three-dimensional frame of solids and voids takes advantage of every opportunity to bask in the sunlight.

Ornamental wood blocks inside help to bounce the light into dark corners and to blunt the glare between the bright outdoors and the softly lighted interior. Ranks of wood slats and free-hanging chains and ropes add texture to the flat plywood sides and echo the filigree of tree limbs and leaves in the surrounding woods.

The Overstreet house successfully subverts the cube. Wresting the pure form from conventional modernism, the architecture softens the cubic geometries with natural materials and textures, giving the light boxes the feeling of a walk in woods.

This house of poles lifts its rooms above the hill overlooking part of San Francisco Bay. At right is a trellis that covers an outdoor dining gazebo, which is linked to the kitchen by a bridge. Two light boxes pop above the roofline to capture light for the house's interior. Vines tie the house to the wooded hillside; a fish pond is in the foreground.

ABOVE The exposed timber structure sets a regular rhythm, while furniture focuses
conversation, dining and viewing areas. Subdued indirect illumination permits the
distant hillside lights into the house. The modules and crafted wood frames of the
Japanese *tonsu* chests bear a striking similarity to the architecture.
OPPOSITE An overhead light box filters sunlight. Wood-trim ornament bounces
and reflects light to balance the contrast between light and shadow; grilles open into
the dining room.

ABOVE A slate roof sweeps up from the intimate one-story master bedroom suite (right) to the two-level guest wing (left); the dining room and kitchen terrace are in the middle. The row of outriggers along the roof's edge is a skylight that allows light into the master bathroom.

Kendrick Kellogg

Rancho California House, California

This house (1988) creates its own landscape of forests and mesas, of tree canopies and weathered rock thrusting up out of the earth's surface. The hovering, winglike roof is held aloft on wooden poles, which support the laminated-wood beams that form the underskeleton of the plank ceiling. Skylights at the intersection of the three distinct copper-trimmed roof plates allow light into the house.

The topography of this landscape is varied and dramatic, with ramps and cascading steps connecting one level to another. Woven between the forest of poles are stone walls, warped and twisting in form, constructed of concrete and covered in fist-sized rocks. They are laid up like a jigsaw puzzle, but not one has been cut to fit and they retain their natural rough edges. The living area's focal point is a vast freestanding spire of stone – an abstract pinnacle that pierces the roof's plane and forms the fireplace and chimney.

The arrangement of interior space is guided by the experience of living, not by an artificial geometry of inorganic grids. The master bedroom takes up one wing of the 6600-square-foot house, with a garden bath and dressing area. At the center of the house is the intimate family room and kitchen. Three guest rooms are on an upper level reached via a ramp that wraps around this core. It is a house as spacious as all outdoors – but also as intimate and varied.

ABOVE LEFT A fantasia of natural forms: the great free-standing fireplace, covered in a mosaic of fist-sized stones, rises like a desert pinnacle in the home's living room. The roof is held aloft by wooden poles, like a canopy above a forest; its three planes are separated by a skylight running the length and breadth of the house.

Rooted in the ground yet soaring skyward, the house seems to float above
the landscape on its winglike roof spans. The main entrance is by a pool;
the terrace overlooking a small lake is to the left.

BELOW The most dramatic view of the
house is from the hill opposite.
OPPOSITE Laminated wood columns rising
from the house's central hub turn and
become the beams that support the roof's
varying levels. The kitchen, living room and
study – each on a different level – extend
beyond the glass walls on cantilevered
decks.

Kendrick Kellogg
Moonlight House, La Jolla, California

As one enters the residence, it seems to drop away
beneath your feet. The spaces are held aloft on platforms
that spiral down and away, following the plunging line
of the steep hillside on which the house is perched.
From the kitchen at the highest point, the living room,
outdoor terrace, study and the bedrooms beyond each
step down around the core. No walls are needed to
separate one living area from another. The carefully
designed space does that.

Freed from the tyranny of the conventional roof and
wall, of window and corridors, the house gives us a secure
foothold at the same time as it opens us to the possibilities
of free-flowing space. The panoramic view of the hillsides
and valley beyond remains a constant. Even the fireplace,
the traditional solid heart of a house, has a window, a link
to the outdoors.

Starting in a sinewy cluster in a small central garden
at the heart of the house, laminated wood columns
shoot upward like a fountain, gracefully curving over,
wavelike, to form the roof. More like an animal's ribs than
a framework, the beams cantilever out at the edge into
wide eaves edged in copper and turned up slightly like
a wing tip, leaving only sheets of glass, the simplest
enclosure possible, to form the outer wall.

No corners. No walls. Space is contained and made
useful with a few suggestive and well-placed strokes
of structure, like a Japanese brush painting. It's not always
obvious how the architect has done it – but the feeling
of both solid protection and utter spatial freedom
is masterful.

Kendrick Kellogg

Westway House, La Jolla, California

ABOVE Overlooking the Pacific Ocean,
this Southern Californian house and its
terraces ramble along the natural contours
of the steep hill.

BELOW RIGHT From the street much of
the house is concealed. The flat roof is held
up by its own structure of columns. Because
supporting walls are not needed, they are
free to be shaped organically by the
residents' needs.

The house is located in a typical, upmarket California oceanside neighborhood. The residences – mostly custom designs – sit side by side on narrow roads winding along the irregular hillside. Each has a magnificent ocean view, each is a private world. But Kendrick Kellogg went a step further to bring the private world of his clients into harmony with the natural world.

From the street the house (1979) might easily be missed, but once one is secluded behind its walls, the panoramic view of sky and ocean opens up magnificently. Contained with a high wall, the courtyard melds into the interior spaces. The house wraps around the hillside clinging close to the ground. The main living area is lined with glass. Structural columns step aside to create living areas.

Kellogg's work is in many ways closer to landscape architecture than what we usually think of as building architecture. He is completely at ease with the curvilinear lines of rivers and shorelines, with the crystalline shapes of rock, with the random rhythms of a stroll through a forest clearing. These are the images to which he refers in designing habitations for his clients. He adjusts the structure to the life of the inhabitants, not the other way around.

ABOVE A conservatory of wood and
glass at the entrance extends the house
out from underneath the low, flat roof.
Passing through this secluded area, the
visitor is confronted by the ocean view
at the front door.

RIGHT Under a skylight in the center of
the house is a pivoting glass door, out
of which floor tiles and laminated-wood
roof beams radiate.

Ribbed and roughened cement surfaces add varied textures that help keep flames off the surface. Mica chips embedded in the final paint coat give the walls a pearlescent sheen. Circular bedroom windows on the second floor can be opened for ventilation.

Eugene Tsui

Tsui House, Berkeley, California

It is the same size and height as its neighbors and it is set back the same distance on its plot. But this house (1995) shows that if one begins with entirely different assumptions, one gets a radically different house. Faced with the challenge to make a house that could ride out earthquakes, that reflected the design principles of natural forms and that used materials that are kind to the environment, Tsui ended up where few have gone before.

The house has a strong shell, with sloping walls melting into a curving roof to spread an earthquake's shock evenly through the structure. The round windows, too, have a seismic function: where a tremor's energy travelling through a square structure meets at the corner with wall-cracking force, a curved wall or window is more likely to send the shock-wave smoothly on its way. Between the laminated ribs that form the house's exoskeleton are walls of a lightweight, malleable concrete-and-styrene panel system. Steel mesh sprayed with concrete forms the roof, whose bumps are tubes that cool the house. Put all these concepts together, give them formal expression and you have something more like a living creature than a conventional house.

Beneath the roof is a two-story spiral filled with light. At the bottom is a round area with built-in seating; the dining room, kitchen, outdoor grotto and study flow off this space. A spiralling ramp, suspended from the roof on steel cables tipped with gold lamé, leads up past an oculus, a south-facing dome-shaped window set in a frame of fiberglass and steel. The logic is clear: the tendrils and fins might be suggested by the structure, but it is the architect's imagination that transforms the components into an organic whole.

Biomorphic forms are fully exploited in the concrete
frame. Curving garden walls, at left, lead to the front door,
slightly lower than the sidewalk. The carport is to the right,
behind a translucent plastic curtain – a car can simply drive
through without having to open a garage door. Native
plants that require little water fill in the landscaping.

RIGHT The living room is surrounded by built-in sofas
and a spiral ramp leading to the second-floor bedrooms.
Dime-store colanders embedded in the plaster walls
provide both ornamentation and ventilation for the lights
on the ramps behind.

BELOW LEFT A custom-fabricated window faces south.
The central part is an acrylic-plastic dome set in a frame of
wood and circled by fiberglass strengthened with a steel
reinforcing bar. The spiral ramp hangs on steel cables from
the ring around the skylight above.

BELOW Four pie-shaped, copper-clad pods float up the slope, from the master suite up to children's rooms, guest rooms, offices and indoor pool. Each room has unobstructed views of the landscape in the Rocky Mountains.

Bart Prince

Gradow House, Aspen, Colorado

The 25,000-square-foot Gradow residence (1994) floats above the trees and sloping mountainside like a flotilla of copper-clad observation balloons – which is close to what they are. The curved leading edges of pie-shaped pods afford unobstructed views down the Aspen valley and leave the slope intact.

On the lowest level is the living room, flanked by a half-buried disco and a ballroom; above it hovers the master bedroom suite. Stepping up and back beyond the first pod are the children's rooms, guest rooms and offices. At the highest point, where the house touches the ground once again, are twin indoor lap pools. Enclosed in the winter, the pool room's walls can telescope back in warm weather to create the effect of an outdoor pool.

Usually houses are boxes connected with corridors, but in this free-flowing space the linking spaces had to be reinvented as well. The cavelike main guest entrance at the center of the house leads down to the entertainment areas via a serpentine cascade of stone stairs. The circular concrete cores that lift the pods also contain stairs and elevators, and bridges link one structure to the next. Unexpectedly, the secluded master suite is located just a few steps from the house's main entertainment spaces. The novel circulation system makes the sprawling residence's many parts surprisingly accessible.

RIGHT With panoramic views of the Aspen valley, the living room hugs the ground below the master suite. Steel I-beams support the dramatic cantilevered pods. A revolving bed occupies the projecting bay.

ABOVE Two lap pools on the top floor of the house offer relaxation all year long. When the weather warms, the insulated sandwich-panel walls on either side slide open.

LEFT One wing juts out overhead near the formal guest entry. The house has a "reverse attic": pipes, ventilating equipment and other utilities are carried in the enclosed areas beneath the floors, instead of above them. The trellis covers the outdoor terrace.

More than 250 people have been entertained
at one time in the residence. Just inside
the formal entry, water cascades over the
shimmering surface of a copper-clad
boulder. A screening room is tucked inside.

On the house's lowest level is a welcoming
conversation area in the living room.
In the center is a fireplace set into one of the
concrete tubes that form the structure
and hold the stairs, elevators and utilities.

BELOW The concrete-block library tower, a recent addition, is also a watchtower for looking out to the desert mountains near Albuquerque.

Bart Prince

Prince House, Albuquerque, New Mexico

All houses are the same: a shelter from the sun and rain, a place to greet friends, a kitchen for cooking, a retreat for privacy and calm. Yet when a house radically rethinks how to satisfy these fundamental needs, it challenges our basic assumptions about architecture. Bart Prince's home (1984) begins with these essential requirements, but conceives totally new ways of satisfying them. The floors are not just floors, they also curve up to become walls; the bedrooms become hideaways floating in the tree tops; the living room is a glass tent. By eliminating the hoary cliché of right angles between the ceiling and the wall, the room breaks open and becomes part of the outdoors.

Four hollow concrete towers form the vertical structure. Upper levels sit on channel beams bolted to the columns. For the architect-owner, a studio sits under a spiral roof that skirts a tower on the east end. Decks on the intermediate level provide shade in the hot, high-desert summers. A recent addition is a two-story library in a concrete-block tower with steps that spiral up to access an observation platform.

In the process of rethinking the shape of our houses, the very lives within them can be altered. Even on a standard suburban lot in a typical suburban neighborhood, the ordinary living spaces of a shelter can become extraordinary.

RIGHT Walls, halls, gardens, porches – each convention of architecture is reconsidered and redesigned in this house. The owner-architect's half-buried studio lies beneath the roof, which spirals up out of the earth (foreground), while bedrooms and the study rise above the tree tops on four concrete columns clad in colorful tile.

ABOVE The living room is a glass-roofed tent pitched beneath the shade of the upper floors. It looks out onto a small walled garden that cuts off the house from the typical suburban neighborhood that surrounds it. The kitchen is behind a tiled partition.

OPPOSITE Water-filled tubes regulate heat in the library and music room. The metal filigree entrance passage leads into the living room; the spiral culvert pipe overhead carries ventilating equipment.

A rchitecture of memories, fragments of time and human culture – this is architecture at its most fragile and transcendent. People went west to escape time, to escape the history that in Europe or the American East Coast was often a burden. There, dynamite, bulldozers and political upheaval were required to alter history. History was different in the West. There, the past had been defanged. There, people could pick and choose among the delicacies of history, could select what they liked and deliberately forget what they did not.

While many immigrants unloaded their memories at the Mississippi River – the traditional divide between the American East and West – others checked their cultural baggage through. They proudly displayed their ties to the Old World once they settled on the outer edge of the new one, building in the image of what they remembered. Franciscan friars, among the first Europeans to settle the West, treasured the Baroque grandeur of churches in Mexico and Spain. But when they were re-created in the Western wilderness with adobe instead of stone and Native American labor instead of Europe-trained stone-carvers, memories were transformed as they were made into reality. The powerfully crude mission churches became poor imitations of cathedrals, but superb original designs in their own right. It took another century before a generation of architects realized the kinds of transformations that were possible in the West, and for the first time deliberately exploited them.

That generation was led by Bernard Maybeck, the ideal Western architect-immigrant. A graduate of the Ecole des Beaux Arts in Paris, he knew enough about history to improve on it once he got far enough away from Paris. For Phoebe Apperson Hearst he created Wyntoon, a magical castle, a baronial hall fit for a mountain ruler. For his own house in the Berkeley hills he used tall ceilings and huge windows to turn a tiny one-room cottage into a grand mansion.

Architectural historian Esther McCoy resurrected Maybeck's reputation in 1960 by characterizing him as a grandfather of modernism because of his early and imaginative use of steel sash windows, asbestos boards and concrete. But Maybeck was never interested in modern materials for their own sake; he used them to tell his stories. His expert whimsy is strong prologue to several architects in this section. "In the hands of Maybeck," historian John Beach has written, "the evocation of certain things in the past becomes merely a tool for creating a new sort of visual drama."

the past perfect

part 2

Borrowing from sources as diverse as the gritty traditions of rural farm buildings to the story-book history of Hollywood, Hyperwest architects alter the past to enrich the present. CLOCKWISE FROM TOP LEFT Fleck house by Jonathan Livingston and Roger Fleck, Jordan house by Ace Architects, Quigley penthouse by Rob Wellington Quigley, Tabancay house by Ace Architects.

These houses cover a range of histories. The Feldman house is rooted in geological history, on the most distant fringes of the past. In many parts of the West, the barren desert landscape reveals how the earth has disgorged itself, laid bare the secrets of ancient oceans and shown us the contortions that have shaped the earth's surface. In Yosemite Park, the Four Corners region and the Rocky Mountains, the landscape gives us a glimpse of nature's power. The horizontal stripes of colored rock and the eroded silhouette of the Feldman house draw on this geological history.

Another history involves an individual history. A classic example of this approach is the great Western monument of La Casa Encantada, media baron William Randolph Hearst's make-believe Spanish village designed by Julia Morgan at San Simeon, a town in which the magnificent spired cathedral is, tellingly, his home. On a smaller scale, the Psyllos house connects to the Greek roots of the owner. David Baker's own house is a personal interpretation of the intriguing culture clash between refined uphill cottages and the proletarian stucco boxes of the Berkeley flatlands.

Some houses are based on a history that never was. These go to the heart of history as a cultural artifact, as a way that people have of giving meaning and delight to their lives by telling stories. On the silver screen history is convincingly and realistically told as the story-teller wishes — and often as the popular audience wants to hear it. The fantasy of the Tabancay's turquoise domes and Moorish arches is closer to the movies than to traditional architecture. It's a leap of imagination far beyond the dry ironies of postmodernism. With true affection it expands the repertoire of architecture beyond European classicism.

John Chase's neo-Craftsman bungalow picks up the thread of a style that has been dormant for some time. The Craftsman bungalows of the turn of the century were an innovative Western variation on the ideals of the English Arts and Crafts movement inspired by a new way of life — outdoor living, stripped of tradition and convention, glorifying the exquisite beauty of unadorned native redwood. Yet Chase's design is not a mere imitation: it grasps

the vocabulary of porches and wood joinery and adapts it to a very contemporary project.

Memory's comforting touch is not the only reason for incorporating history into buildings. Ace Architects use history and wit to create spatial grandeur within the unavoidable limits of today's building techniques and budgets. With allusions to Berkeley architecture of the recent past, their Jordan house tells a story with local references, including a Maybeck design for long-gone Hearst Hall and the fairy-tale cottages and witches' hovels seen in the coastal town of Carmel. Little attempt is made to produce anything authentic or exact; that's not the point. The power of this architecture lies in the creative distortion.

Similar preoccupations have shaped the Gregory-Ingraham house, a tour de force of memories and history boldly sculpting the interior space. To the street the house presents the face of an 1890s San Francisco rowhouse by Ernest Coxhead, a contemporary of Maybeck who emigrated from England to California in 1886. Coxhead shared Maybeck's interest in adapting memory to the period and locale. In the 1890s unpainted shingles on a townhouse was as shocking as the corrugated cladding of several of the houses that appear in this book. Jeremy Kotas and Skip Shaffer take Coxhead's rustic-classical shingled façades and blow them up to an enormous size; this house holds probably the world's largest double-hung sash window. The asymmetrical balcony throws the composition off the straight and narrow, skewing the design in a delightfully awkward way, tipping conventions and establishing new rules out of the shards of the old.

From Maybeck through Charles Moore to today's architects with a taste for editing, exaggeration and play, the tradition of historical Hyperwest is well grounded. Richly woven out of the ordinary ways of living, standard contractor construction ignored by the taste-makers of high-art architecture, and with a carefully calibrated awkwardness, these houses of the Western past stake out a deeply popular style. In the warm climate and recent development of the West, nothing seems very permanent. But the enjoyment of time past is still possible in the extraordinary structures that make their own place in history.

Whether in spectacular natural settings or in the midst of dense cities, each of these houses is rooted in the people and places that preceded it.
FROM LEFT Fleck house by Jonathan Livingston and Roger Fleck, Feldman house by Design Group Architects, Psyllos house by Mickey Muennig, Faith's house by Kotas/Pantaleoni.

BELOW Geology is the history of the earth. This house emulates the landscape's colors and strata charting eons of upheaval and erosion. OPPOSITE Irregular forms and angled steps of terraces create a stone mesa out of which crystalline glass shapes emerge.

Design Group Architects

Feldman House, Sedona, Arizona

In the red rock of northern Arizona, the Feldman house (1991) echoes many pasts. The finely laid stone walls and deep-cut openings recall the thousand-year-old architecture of the Anasazi, the ancient people of this region. But the mountains are history, too, a record of the cataclysms and ages of the earth's ever-changing surface, a history laid open throughout the barren Western deserts. The house's horizontal rock walls, shaded from deep red supai sandstone to tan coconino sandstone, mirror the geological strata of the surrounding mountains of Sedona, reflecting a past even deeper than the Anasazi's.

Walking up the irregular stone steps to the house is like a hike up a dry wash running through a landscape carved by innumerable flash floods. The house's silhouette may seem contemporary, jagged, deconstructed, but in fact it matches the contours of the eroding mountains around it. The light and shadow that fall on the bent surfaces vary throughout the day, so from afar the structure seems to blend as seamlessly into the landscape as the natural rock itself. Terrace walls are like small mesas, and the pool by the entrance is a pothole that appears to have been carved into the sandstone by wind and rain and filled with rainwater.

The living room faces the north with broad views of the mountains in protected parkland, ceilings slope upward to take in the panorama; from the outside, they appear to be crystalline outcroppings thrusting up out of a sandstone matrix. By evoking the simply dignity of the Anasazi ruins, the house suggests ways of looking to the West's past to create its future.

OPPOSITE Dry washes are all that remain of vanished streams in the desert landscape. Steps approaching the entrance echo the winding paths of the washes, often encountered during hikes in the surrounding desert. Stone masonry is intricately stacked like the structures of the prehistoric Anasazi culture of the American Southwest.
BELOW RIGHT The entrance side of the house is solid with deep-cut openings, while the opposite, north façade opens up to stunning views of National Forest land.

LEFT Faceted glass walls create the effect of looking
out from inside a prism. The stone fireplace mantel links
the human-scaled foreground with the magnificent
mountains in the distance.

BELOW RIGHT A hexagonal basket-weave pattern of ribs
surrounds a skylight in the raised entrance hall.

Antoine Predock

Fuller House, Carefree, Arizona

BELOW The timeless forms of pyramid and cube are a suitable match for the sublime, immutable desert landscape. OPPOSITE The house's main floor is partially buried in the desert ground, but two open-air pavilions on the east and west ends rise above *palo verde* trees and cactus to act as towers for observing the sunrise and sunset.

Deserts are the natural habitats for mystics, ascetics and hermits. If one chooses to live in the desert, one must acknowledge, one way or another, the special power of the place.

Though it was built in 1987, this seems an ancient house, with overgrowing *palo verde* trees and cactus hiding its walls. On either side of the house two tower lookouts – one for the sunrise, one for the sunset – sheltered by steel trellises rise above the desert vegetation. This is more than a place to live: like the great kivas, the sacred round chambers that Native Americans have carved into the desert floor for a thousand years, something else is intended here.

The sunrise terrace is at the entrance. Next to it the front door is hidden in the gloom at the bottom of some steps. But once inside, water bubbling from a block of stone leads down a thin channel in the floor and out to the light, to the large windows at the far end of the gallery and out to the pool. A long curved wall sweeps alongside through the center of the house, creating the entrance gallery. To one side are the kitchen, breakfast room and dining room, each contained within a separate space, almost like a set of burial rooms in an Egyptian tomb, yet warm and inviting.

The pink stone pyramid outside underscores the residence's mystical aura. Stepped at the bottom, smooth at the top, the pyramid is topped by a clear skylight. Inside is a study, but the outside of the form enhances the house's presence against the awesome desert setting.

RIGHT A stone pyramid with a smooth-faced and
stepped surfaces dominates the pool. Within is a study
skylit by the glass tip. An indoor fountain acts as a water
source that leads from the front door, along a narrow
channel cut into the foyer-gallery floor, through the wall
and out into the circular pool. Metal screens with
a classical Roman pattern provide shade.
BELOW Saguaro cactus, native to Arizona, and other
desert flora densely clustered around the house convey
the atmosphere of an ancient ruin.

BELOW Domes, minarets and guardian dragons re-create a Moorish palace that never existed – but should have – in the hills of Oakland.

OPPOSITE Seen from the second-story balcony, the blue floor dappled with spiralling gold ceramic tile mirrors the night sky, which can be seen through the skylight overhead. The four Moorish-Gothic columns display an opulence well beyond their origins as ordinary steel drainage pipes.

Ace Architects

Tabancay House, Oakland, California

A Moorish fantasy of harems and opulence, of gem-studded walls and turquoise onion domes piercing the azure sky, of forest views glimpsed through the filigree of Byzantine trefoils – the fabled Orient (or more truthfully, the fable *of* the Orient) has been transported to the Oakland hills. It is a dream world many times removed from fact, closer to Hollywood than Granada. No matter: it still inspires wondrous spaces.

The hills around Oakland have a long tradition of magnificence on the cheap. Throughout the West there is a tradition of builder-contractors who have created neighborhoods chock-a-block with humble stucco bungalows, which – with a minimal tower entry and an appropriate roofline – could be sold as a Moorish, Tudor or Navajo fantasy.

In the same spirit Ace Architects conjure a Thousand-and-One-Nights palace out of the simplest of materials in a house they built in 1990. The blue domes are off-the-shelf items used to cap farm silos. Where modernists might have used the cap for its functionality, here it has been used for its exotic iconography.

The domes, tiles and pointed arches are used to create great spaces: a living room with the colors and shapeliness of the Alhambra, tile screens that dematerialize walls into graphic patterns, columns and perspectives that compress a series of magnificent halls into a few short feet. The forms are bold and affectionate, not ironic; the shapes are instantly identifiable and iconic, never fussily authentic. Architecture is an expressive art, and when it embraces diversity, it soars. Akbar the Great would never have been fooled – but he would have had fun.

ABOVE The dining table and chairs, as well as the sideboard mirror, were all designed using the same iconic Moorish forms as the house's architecture – a perfect marriage of architecture and craft.

RIGHT The informal breakfast area off the kitchen enjoys morning sun filtered through the hillside forest and the twisted pillars.

OPPOSITE A colonnade of pointed Moorish arches is only the width of a bench, but adds depth to the living room. Ceramic tiles splash the wall with color and pattern to ornament the fireplace.

Ace Architects

Jordan House, Oakland, California

The urban forest fire that consumed Dixie Jordan's first house and scores of neighboring houses in 1991 swept away all her possessions. The only thing the inferno left was memories. Happily for her, Lucia Howard and David Weingarten of Ace Architects find memories as good as plywood, glass and concrete for design. When they designed a replacement house for her in 1993, they built solidly on her remembrances – and added a few of their own.

What resulted is not an imitation of what was there before, however. The house's style draws on a splendid assortment of historical buildings in the area, from the cottages of Berkeley architect Bernard Maybeck and his noble 1899 Hearst Hall at the nearby University of California campus (long since razed), to firehouses and other sly bits and charming pieces.

The outcome of this cut-and-paste approach is a small cottage that seems to remember a grand previous life. The roof shoots upward to create a lofty central living area illuminated by pendant lights whose Gothic lines echo the roofline. A majestic balcony elbows its way into the space overlooking the living room in case the local baron decides to reclaim the house and give a speech to his minions. Magnificent doors let out onto a tiny terrace.

The promise of the West is that one can create one's own world. The Jordan house creates its own past and its own future. Though historical wit pervades the house, it is far from a one-line joke. With color and meticulous distortions of scale, it creates a grandeur rarely achieved in most larger houses. It is a proclamation that history is a mandatory building material.

BELOW The original Jordan house and its hillside neighborhood were destroyed by a disastrous urban forest fire in 1991.
OPPOSITE Despite the house's small size, the architecture magnifies certain features to convey confidence and grandeur, as in the trellis on the kitchen terrace.

LEFT The stair landing is a romantic balcony squeezed onto palace-size brackets overlooking the living room. The wood railing and the pierced-copper pendant lamps hanging from the ceiling echo the house's pointed-arch motif. The stairs to the left ascend to the kitchen; stairs to the right go nowhere at all.

BELOW The drama of the soaring wood beams is underscored by the clerestory light high above the living room. Historicist details highlighted by vivid colors can be seen in materials that evoke the local architectural craft traditions.

LEFT The Gothic-vaulted living room and its terrace (right) balance the flat-roofed bedroom tower and its balcony (left). Dragon-head trellis beams guard the front door. Copper-coated shingles cover the roof and are repeated over the mantel inside.

Mickey Muennig

Psyllos House, Big Sur, California

Big Sur is one of the wild places in North America. Ragged mountains crash into a violent Pacific, while homesteads nestle in redwood groves at the bottom of canyons or cling to windswept cliffs overlooking the ocean. For the ridge-top Psyllos house (1985), Mickey Muennig borrowed the whitewashed walls and soft forms of villages found along another wild sea, the Aegean, to create a place of protection. The owner has Greek roots and liked the idea of echoing those traditional villages in this far-away place.

The north walls of the house wrap around the outdoor terraces like sheltering arms to ward off the prevailing northwest winds, and the entire house is half buried into the hill. But to the south it is a house of glass, opening to the views and the sunlight.

The house spills down the hill, with a meandering marble stairway that hugs the slope's contours like a river bed and functions as the house's spine. From the top level to bottom, the living room, kitchen and bedrooms all open off the spine. Sod terraces cover the exposed rooftops and extend the bedrooms into the outside. Stark white walls stand out dramatically from the hills' greens and browns, but the flowing forms and planted roofs tie the house closely to the earth.

ABOVE LEFT The house is carved into the hillside, but the open western face is mostly glass looking out over the Pacific Ocean.
LEFT From the uphill side, the sod-covered roofs blend with the mountain as it falls gently away to the surf far below. The garage roof is the foreground; the kitchen is to the right, the living room to the left.
OPPOSITE Just inside the front door, green marble steps cascade down a natural cleft in the slope. Rooms are entered off this spine, from the living room at the top to the private guest and family rooms on lower levels. Cut and fitted concrete blocks covered with white stucco form the long arches.

ABOVE The house's three vaulted structures are clustered together, recalling the white-plaster-clad villages of the Aegean islands. Entrance is on the left into a walled courtyard. The living room, at right, opens onto the pool terrace.
OPPOSITE The two-story vault makes room for a loft space above and bedroom below. All three buildings are linked by underground passages. Roofs are covered in white ceramic tile.

Wallace Cunningham

Ganymede House, Del Dios, California

The sloping white walls and vaulted roofs of this house (1985) recall a village by the Aegean Sea. Three barrel-vaulted structures, clad in tiles, sit at neat right angles to each other. The spaces between are carefully considered: walled courts, cascades of stairs and a pool terrace create paths and plazas that run between the simple buildings. With a few chairs set beneath it, a spreading olive tree in the main court serves as a pleasant outdoor waiting room for a home office that has a separate entrance.

Unseen from the outside, however, are underground passageways that link the village-like cluster of edifices into one sprawling house of private hideaways and generous entertainment areas. The main door is in the glass-filled end of one vault, and the entrance winds down around a zig-zag chimney that anchors one side of the long living room. If the living room is the village's chapel, the chimney is its altar.

The living room is also the central concourse of the house, the point off which the other wings radiate. The stairs wrapping around the tall fireplace lead down a short tunnel into one wing, which includes a bedroom and a loft under the gently arching ceiling. Off the living room in the other direction a large open kitchen doubles as an underground tunnel to the four-level wing. A spiralling staircase leads up, first to the office-study level off the main court, and then up to two secluded hideaways.

Historically, a village is a place where one can socialize in public or retreat into privacy. With its collection of open terraces and hidden cloistered spaces, the Ganymede residence offer a microcosm of the same possibilities.

ABOVE The front door (left) is secondary to the unspoiled view of the lake.
LEFT The owners can collect and process the olives from a tree in the graveled
entrance court that doubles as a pleasant waiting room for the home-office.

BELOW Faceted, butt-jointed glass next to the front door encloses one end of the living room structure. The glass is continued inside as a transparent railing. OPPOSITE The living room fireplace anchors stairs up to the front door (left) and stairs down to a passageway that leads to one wing (right).

TOP Barns are a familiar sight in the rolling dairyland north of San Francisco.
ABOVE The round storage structure mirrors the grain bins of farm
compounds. A band of clerestory windows runs just under the ridge gable.

Jonathan Livingston (architect) with Roger Fleck
Fleck House, Nicasio, California

Barns dot the dairylands just north of San Francisco. The familiar form – a long gabled roof with a raised ridge, another gable at right angles in the center that completes a cruciform shape – evolved out of a barn's function long ago and was used again and again for its simple construction.

It was the form that caught the eye of industrial designer Roger Fleck and triggered the design of his combined house, office and workshop, built in 1990. Under half of the roof lies a roomy house, with a bedroom and office in the loft. The other half is a workshop for Fleck's design business. The spacious living area is informal, with dining and conversation areas at the perimeter and a kitchen at the center, beneath the open bedroom loft.

But there are changes to the barn formula. Instead of the conventional wood frame, this barn is framed in steel and bolted together by hand. Where a wood barn's frame is thick and a bit ragged, steel is light, tense and precise. The change in materials highlights the classical form of the vernacular barn; the side aisles and soaring ridgeline are those of a classical basilica; light pouring in through the clerestory windows under the ridge spreads an even and beautiful light.

Cedar planks clad the exterior and metal covers the roof. Inside plywood panels backed with insulation fill in the exposed structure. Floors are burnished concrete in the kitchen and Philippine aptong wood in the living areas.

The historic form of the barn still blends with the rolling landscape, but here it has been sharpened and clarified in the way a still-life painting enriches for us the color, texture and form of an inanimate object. It allows us to see the ordinary as extraordinary.

A steel frame and cedar-plank siding give the barn a crisp, machine-honed appearance not found in older, vernacular wood barns. Barn doors roll sideways to afford views from the living part of the house (left). The owner's workshop occupies the structure's other half.

ABOVE Commercial store-front windows frame the view.
Flooring is finished concrete; the line of boxes over the
window contains stereo speakers. Throughout the building
the steel structure is exposed.

RIGHT The bedroom loft overlooks the main living area.
A steel frame, bolted in place, gives the space a light and
airy appearance.

LEFT The living part of the house is one large space
flooded with light. A loft contains the master bedroom
and bath. Below is the kitchen behind corrugated wall;
a conversation area is to left. The private guest room is
beyond the back wall of kitchen.

ABOVE The same steel structure that adds clean lines to the living half of
the building is functional and efficient in the workshop half. The resident
can oversee operations from the second-level office.

OPPOSITE The office has enough workspace for employees and views of
the hillside through the ribbon of glass just under the gable eaves.

BELOW The house grew out of a second story that had been left uncompleted above a San Francisco residence for more than eighty years. The bay window faces the Golden Gate Bridge. OPPOSITE Exposed structure and rectilinear forms reveal the modernist influence on the house – but only on the exterior. Translucent infill lets the stair structure stand out.

Ira Kurlander

Kurlander House, San Francisco, California

Liberated from the constraints of tasteful authenticity, Ira Kurlander designed a house in 1980 that recalls classical remnants without falling into the trap of historical correctness, proving that a house can create its own time and space. With murals, moldings and *faux* drapery, he creates a penthouse with the delightful atmosphere of an open-air garden in an idyllic time, a memory from an invented past. The fresh sea-breeze always seems to drift through the casually draped curtains that encircle the main living space. The northern view of the Golden Gate Bridge may be shrouded in fog, but the southern view, painted on the wall, will always be sunlit and clear.

The fireplace mantle does double duty in the small house as a stair to the upper-level bedroom suite. Reached by a glass-enclosed stairway, the penthouse sits atop the structure as if it landed there like a dirigible. To complete the thought, the guest room and bath are fitted out in a spare metallic style, like a cabin on the Graf Zeppelin. The dining room and kitchen, encased in windows, have the ambience of a schooner, and while the vision of an open-air terrace is only an illusion, the feeling is real.

Look at this house one way and it's all wrong: the historicist interior clashes with the modernist exterior, the classical ornament thumbs its nose at Vitruvius. But look at it another way, it succeeds: it's not about slavish authenticity, it's about creating a marvelous place.

ABOVE Trompe-l'oeil mural of steps and sky turn the
penthouse into a roof garden.

RIGHT Curving curtains – made of wood – that hang
in each corner transform the square living room into
a focussed, intimate circular room. Historical forms and
decorations actually shape the space, rather than merely
ornamenting it.

LEFT The fireplace and mantel turn a playful face to the
living room, an ideal space for entertaining. Egyptian
obelisks, Ionic capitals and Renaissance pediments are
each used in unexpected ways. The stairs to the left wrap
around the chimney and lead to the upstairs bedroom.

TOP Off-kilter eyebrows, asymmetrical balcony and an over-sized window hint that it may not be all that it appears to be.
ABOVE Inside, the house explodes as a single multifaceted space with a rollicking collage of shapes, materials and levels. A metal ramp bridges the library to the bedroom.

Jeremy Kotas and Skip Shaffer
Gregory-Ingraham House, San Francisco, California

This house is a time machine. At its center lies a vortex that splits the 1989 residence in half. Every day, on the way to feeding the cat or picking up the mail, the owners meet and greet past and future, Queen Victoria and Buck Rogers, and travel from garden to city, from solid darkness to airy light.

The casual visitor would call that vortex the stairwell that rises through the house. It begins in a darkened entry, a perfect Edwardian picture gallery of classical moldings and deeply shadowed tints of maroon, royal blue and red. It leads to a flight of wood steps that are squeezed out into the light of a fragmentary Victorian greenhouse with tall windows looking over a miniature fern garden. Tracing an oval spiral through the house's six distinct levels, the stairs lead to the high-rise living room, a dramatic view of the San Francisco skyline and to the kitchen, which opens onto a wilderness garden.

Here the solid wood stairs begin to break apart, turning first into floating slabs, then becoming metal treads that cantilever precariously off a tipping wall, like something out of a 1950s sci-fi movie. The stairs ascend to the upper level of the living room's library wall before traversing a steel gangplank to a Bedroom of Tomorrow with movable closets and aluminum-sheathed bathroom pods. Its slanting walls and flashes of skylight are centuries away from the upright Edwardian gloom of the entrance – but from the railing you can look down, through the near past into the distant past, all contained in this simple shingled row house.

OPPOSITE The library is an entire wall (at left) of the two-story living room. The kitchen is on the other side of the stairwell; above it, the bedroom wall has been cut away. The corrugated cylinder forms part of the dressing room.

ABOVE A spiral stair whirls through the center of the house. Tall
conservatory windows on the lower level overlook a small garden.
The entrance foyer is to the right.

OPPOSITE Randomly scattered skylights flood the house's core with
light, dividing it into the living room and library wings (left) and the kitchen
and bedroom wing (right). The stairs change character as they rise;
cantilevered steel treads link the kitchen to the library, while a steel-mesh
ramp connects the library to the bedroom.

John Chase (architect) with Claudia Carol and David Henry Jacobs
Jacobs Studio, Santa Monica, California

This 1988 studio-guesthouse displays all the hallmarks of a classic Craftsman bungalow: shady porches, board-and-batten walls, exposed wood eaves outside and trusses inside. It is almost fanatically correct, but it veers away from being an imitation. How? This is a living, breathing Californian bungalow created long after historians thought they were dead.

Chase understands perfectly the Craftsman love of wood joinery and patterns, but he also captures the rustic eccentricity, the freedom and play of the bungalows that made them so livable. A few Craftsman bungalows were mansions, like the Gamble house by Greene and Greene in Pasadena, but the vast majority were tiny, like this one.

The site is much too small for a structure that needs to hug the ground with porches and walls – yet each of the four façades rambles with offhanded ease. A miniaturized window bay, deftly off-balance amid the facade's overall symmetry, makes the house appear bigger than it is. Inside this loft-sleeping porch (in a small house everything must have two functions) awakening sleepers must have the feeling of being Alice on her Wonderland Ever-Gro diet.

The spaciousness of a much larger bungalow is created in a single room by a fireplace wall, a masterpiece of compressed design. Within a two-foot depth the fireplace mantle warps the wall into a window seat, fireplace, window bay and a fragment of an overhead truss. Large doors to the front porch on one side and the dining deck on the other draw the outside inside in appropriate Southern California Craftsman style. Liberties with traditional styles were taken here, but they've paid off handsomely.

ABOVE Doubling as a studio and guest apartment, every spare corner is used: the sleeping loft (right) is set on top of a storage area; a glass-enclosed bathroom shares light with the rest of the bungalow.

OPPOSITE, ABOVE The wood frame grid shows through, highlighted by asymmetrical windows, clapboarding of varying sizes and a pop-out sleeping loft. Small-scale windows and oversized base boards playfully confuse the apparent size.

OPPOSITE, BELOW The fireplace wall incorporates seating areas, cabinets, windows and gallery, all in a lively composition.

Robert Overstreet (architect), Jim Jennings (interiors)
Oliver Ranch House, Geyserville, California

The Oliver ranch house (1986) uses the sturdy simple shapes of a traditional Western ranch house and melts them into the golden grass meadows, the wide oaks and the rock outcroppings of Sonoma County, one of the principal wine regions of California. As a historic type the ranch house usually had a large fireplace built to brace occupants against the cold, with hand-hewn logs as wall material. The comfort and appeal of this image was later scaled up to public spaces and celebrated in the grand lobbies of rustic National Park hotels, like the Old Faithful Inn in Wyoming's Yellowstone Park, and the Ahwanee Hotel in California's Yosemite Park.

This modern ranch house re-creates those lodges on the residential scale. Simple gabled roofs top the house and its wings; inside the ceiling of the four-square living room rises high, supported by four round, rustic columns, while redwood rafters rhythmically criss-cross the ceiling.

For modern living, an elegant kitchen has been added, a white box slipped into the barn-like living space. The open living spaces are differentiated by subtle inflections in levels – a raised podium for the dining area, an open area in front of the large concrete fireplace. Simplified but glorified, the ranch house tradition continues today.

ABOVE LEFT The rolling countryside of Sonoma County provides the backdrop for this hilltop house, set in a 100-acre ranch. A pool terrace rests on top of the stepped landscaping.
LEFT At the main entrance, the stone landscape appears to grow out of the ground to support the walls and copper roof. Overscaled column bases match boulders in size. A cupola marks the central living space, with bedroom wings angled off it.

ABOVE LEFT Window mullions accent the
gently arched windows. The dining area sits on
an elevated podium overlooking the living room.
ABOVE RIGHT A massive concrete fireplace,
the focal point of the living room, repeats the
arch motif that recurs throughout the house.

Kotas/Pantaleoni (architects), Joanne Koch (associate)
Faith's House, San Francisco, California

Entire districts of little box houses rise and fall with the hills of San Francisco. They are modest, compact, nestled wall to wall on small lots, with virtually identical floor plans. Yet each maintains an individual sense of dignity because each has its own street face. On any given block one might encounter haciendas, châteaux, streamlined townhouses or 1950s ranch houses.

This last style is what Jeremy Kotas has appropriated for a house, built in 1992, in a typical neighborhood. It has the same garage below and the same main floor above as its neighbors. It has a bay window to capture light on foggy days and the flat roof popular in 1950s Bay Area modernism, but then the bay window goes rubbery and flexible so that the house can crane its neck out to get a good view of the distant Bay Bridge. And, in the back, instead of meekly facing its small backyard, the house shifts on its haunches and takes a good look out at the view. With this slight architectural maneuver, the house claims for itself its own yard, its neighbors' yards and the house-covered hills beyond.

Inside, the rooms continue the spare, dynamic lines of 1950s modernism. The living-room ceiling sweeps upward, and diagonal pylons frame the windows. Skylights flood the entry hall. The walls wrap around a column and then flip into an elegant late Moderne curve that leads smoothly into the kitchen wall.

Even from the simplest mass-produced houses a tradition can grow. Faith's house shows that tradition's potential for delight, comfort and personality.

Row after row of simple homes, with garages on the ground floor and living areas raised to the second floor, make up much of the San Francisco cityscape. Some are Spanish, some château-style, some Moderne to give each house a measure of individuality. In details such as the flat roof eaves and canted window frames, this residence draws inspiration from the modern vernacular of contractor-built houses of the 1950s. Stained plywood and painted stucco are complemented by the luminous plastic sheet over the front door. Bold colors bring out the simplicity of the forms.

ABOVE Curving walls in the living room at the front and in the kitchen at
the back form an s-curve that ties the main floor together. A single window
framing a distant landmark for diners at the kitchen table was added during
construction, when the view was revealed through the unfinished walls.
RIGHT The master bathroom features glass block, colorful hard plastic walls
and custom cabinetry that emphasize the house's bold colors and shapes.
OPPOSITE Three living room windows angle out to capture a view of the
San Francisco Bay Bridge. The diagonal lines of the window columns were
a common feature of 1950s modern design in the West.

BELOW With its pattern of secondary rafters and tie rods, the exposed wood ceiling recalls the San Francisco Bay Area's Craftsman tradition.

David Baker and Nancy Whitcombe
Baker House, Berkeley, California

An architect who builds his own house designs it from his personal history. It may overlap with a history shared by other people, but the key to the visual puzzle of the Baker house (1992) is the eye that designed it. Just as the West was hammered together by people from different origins, eras and outlooks, this house borrows pieces from everywhere. The floating kitchen counter is a 1950s-style amoeba shape seen in the best drive-ins and coffee shops; the righteous brick fireplace is a stray from a neighboring Craftsman house in Berkeley; the perforated aluminum benches lining the terrace could be descendants of a tractor seat; the shapely chromed legs on the bathroom sink seem to have walked off a Chippendale chair.

From the outside the forms seem piled up, like an artistic train wreck. Inside, the rooms interpenetrate on multiple levels, spatially mirroring the exterior. Throughout the West benign climates make stucco irresistible to builders, but Baker refers to the house as the "Revenge of the Stuccoids," the cheap but intriguing wood-framed and stucco-clad houses and apartments common in the flat part of Berkeley. The clash of gray Portland cement stucco with the warm and woodsy trellises and ceilings charges the house with wit and energy.

All these pieces are put together still alive, still wiggling and swaying like the tree branches outside. The past is alive and well.

RIGHT Fragments of colliding stucco rhomboids and wood cubes give the house a jaunty energy. The multilevel interior, with its many terraces and views, is as interwoven and unexpected as the forms piling up outside suggest. The deck is lined with perforated metal benches; the syncopated trellis beams radiate out from a point inside the house.

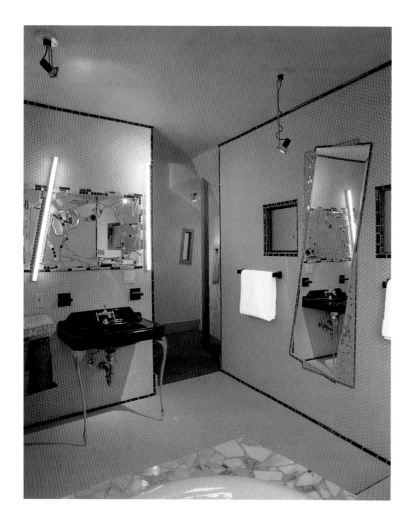

LEFT The bathroom is a play with the concussive lines of colliding objects and shattered stone, tempered by inlaid seashells and multicolored tiles.

RIGHT The kitchen cutting board and stove-top are clamped to steel structural columns and can be raised or lowered to match any chef's comfort. In contrast to this industrial efficiency, the brick fireplace seems to be a fragment out of the past – which it is, borrowed from the vernacular bungalows of turn-of-the-century Berkeley.

BELOW The top of a five-story office
building has become an urban hacienda
for the architect and his family. Twin
towers are used for storage, but with
masts and cylindrical forms framed by
a courtyard wall they become an
intriguing landmark against the sky.
OPPOSITE With his office one floor
below, the commute is easy; with the
articulated shapes of a penthouse, the
building's silhouette becomes an antidote
to the typical flat-roofed high-rise.

Rob Wellington Quigley
Quigley Penthouse, San Diego, California

The romance of living outdoors is rooted deeply in
the West's past. Author Helen Hunt Jackson captured
the romance in her 1884 story, *Ramona*, a tale of benighted
love in the haciendas of Spanish Catholic California.
The golden myth was played out in the hacienda
courtyards, where daily life in the temperate climate
was lived, where meals were cooked in adobe fireplaces,
where church affairs and genteel gossip were discussed
in tree-shaded patios.

Part of the myth is true. The climate was paradise;
it still is in Southern Californian cities. The air is warm, and
living, eating and relaxing outdoors is as easy here as
anywhere on earth. Rob Wellington Quigley continues
the idyll of the hacienda in his own home with a modest
adaptation to the present: this courtyard residence, built
in 1988, is in a penthouse atop a five-story office building
in a funky bayside neighborhood of San Diego.

The rooms of the house are arranged around a large
part of the patio in a free-flowing space. Glass walls
become doors that pivot open; furniture can be wheeled
in or out to make the outside part of the living space.
The courtyard is enclosed by a stucco wall, inset with a
fireplace. A slice of the view of the old Art Déco city hall
and the bay beyond is tantalizingly visible over a bower
of bougainvillea and greenery.

Quigley's hacienda is not adobe, however. The stucco
coat is industrial gray, the flooring is recycled tire rubber.
Twin towers topped with spires and aircraft warning lights
loom overhead as a beacon to the future. This courtyard is
in the present, not the past, but it will take the centuries-old
tradition of outside living into the future.

LEFT Glass walls open from each room
onto the circular courtyard, a boon in
the balmy San Diego climate. The glass
pyramids in the foreground are skylights
to the office below. Heavy-duty indoor-
outdoor flooring is made of recycled
rubber tires.

RIGHT The breakfast room takes full
advantage of the in-town site with glass
walls that look out over the old bay-side
city hall. A fabric canopy can be pulled
over the courtyard.

Consider the corrugated metal panel. A slick product of twentieth-century technology and mass production, it was used by lonely prospectors to build shacks in the desert. Originally a utilitarian blue-collar material, it became a signature device for any building that wanted to be high-tech. This dual character perfectly describes the nature of technology in general in the West: pragmatic, functional, popular, corporate, standardized, do-it-yourself, liberating, absolutely necessary and omnipresent.

The pioneers and boomers who created the West jerry-built an uneasy working relationship between machines and the landscape. If nature could bless, it could also turn murderous, so their only defense was machinery. From Conestoga wagons to railroads to jets, from dams to cable cars to aerospace, technology is our weapon against heat, lack of water, alkaline soil, lonely distances and thirst. Machines became heroic when water from the Sierra Nevada and Rocky Mountains was piped hundreds of miles to Los Angeles, San Francisco, Phoenix and other desert cities. Finally, the automobile changed the way people lived forever, and Los Angeles became the first city in history designed for the car. A mythology of technology and its fruits grew as a result of these technical advances. Machines did not just serve the basic need for shelter from the elements and protection from danger; they provided ease and comfort, oases in the wilderness, nirvanas that transformed humble lives into something more than mere existence.

If organic architecture optimistically embraces nature, technowest is somewhat more wary. But it uses nature to its advantage. In two houses in different climes, Steve Badanes coerces harsh climates to create comfortable habitations: the Baja house is essentially a machine, cooling and shading itself with a wind-scoop roof; in the Hill house passive solar-heating technology soaks up the sun for the owner's use.

Other technowest buildings invest meaning in machine-made materials. David Ireland's high-walled shed in San Francisco subtly shifts corrugated metal away from its vernacular roots with studied proportions. Jim Jennings uses it in high-art fashion, as an aesthetic texture, color and surface, contrasting it with sleek concrete panels in a conscious duality of form and texture. Here, simple geometries and industrial finishes follow the long tradition of the Case Study houses of the post-World War II era.

technowest

part 3

Technology is celebrated in the shapes, surfaces and the very presence of these houses in inhospitable locations.
UPPER LEFT AND LOWER RIGHT Malibu house by Edward Niles.
UPPER RIGHT Sidley house by Edward Niles.
LOWER LEFT Ireland house by David Ireland.

William Bruder returns the wavy metallic surfaces to their blue-collar roots. The shiny trapezoidal volumes covered in galvanized metal at the Hill-Sheppard house have the boxy populist appearance of a mobile-home parking lot. The house's wings are carefully parked on the site to create three distinct courtyards on a tight urban lot. Some details have the pragmatic directness of folk art; others are intriguingly complex. Both exist comfortably side by side.

Though corrugated metal has crossed over into respectability, asphalt shingles have not. A mealy, mottled mass-produced material, it still has the smell of lower-class remodels. Modernists can appreciate corrugated tin for its clean metallic finish and its sine-curve surface, but asphalt shingles are an imitative aesthetic: their color and shape are a cheap simulation of honest wood shingles, telling a popular story of bourgeois domesticity. Even Frank Gehry's use of asphalt shingles for his own house (they were found objects, after all) could not raise its acceptance level. Rob Wellington Quigley's Capistrano glass house, however, bravely takes on the asphalt shingle and its overtones of a cultural vernacular, displaying them aggressively as a foil to a beefy concrete structure. He even invites them into the master bedroom. The shingles are not used for any abstract industrial beauty, though. Like the seminal modernist R.M. Schindler, Quigley broadens architecture to include all the cheap materials and shacky glories of the ordinary contractor vernacular.

Technowest's moment of transcendence arrived with the opening of Hoover Dam in 1936. Holding back millions of gallons of water for reliable irrigation and hydroelectric generation, even today the dam is an engineering wonder. Thirty miles from Las Vegas, the dam rises in a barren landscape of jagged mountains and deeply shadowed canyons. But the dam gains elegance by its architectural flourishes, designed by Los Angeles architect Gordon Kaufmann. He used not the industrially based International Style, but the Streamline Moderne style, the commercial interpretation of the machine age seen in drive-in restaurants and gas stations across the nation, and especially on the strips of the West. To use such a popular aesthetic

might have cheapened the dam to a period piece, but instead it bestowed dignity and grandeur.

Technology in all its manifestations finds its way into technowest architecture. Daring engineering feats and mass-produced materials are all part of this tradition, a lode which Western architects fruitfully mine. The trestle-like bridge-deck at Antoine Predock's Zuber house in Paradise Valley, Arizona, recalls the industrial landscape of the railroad. It is an odd shape and an odd place for a deck, long and thin and projecting into mid-air at an angle to the house, but it ties the house to the human landscape in all its facets.

John Lautner and Edward Niles also seek to redeem corporate technology. Niles uses standard off-the-shelf steel sections that are the common vocabulary of office parks everywhere in the United States. His doors, windows and glass skins are also standard. He takes these regimented materials of corporate America and twists and pulls them until they have something to say about humanity, about nature. Their shiny surfaces actively debate with the dry, red earth and jagged mountains of Malibu. Lautner, on the other hand, used technology to replicate the realms where humans first sought shelter eons ago: caves, forests, rocks and mountains. His buildings are as technically sophisticated as Niles's, but instead of standing in sharp contrast to their rugged settings, they echo the landscape. At heart Lautner was always an engineer, using walls of glass that slide back at the flick of a switch, voice-operated doors and daring cantilevers, and yet he always kept a humanist perspective about technology. At the Sheats-Goldstein house he has created a crystalline cave of concrete. It is made of a twentienth-century materials, but it has the feeling of one of humankind's ancestral homes.

Humans do not always succeed in the West, but when individuals and groups have, it has usually been because they had tools in their hands. No wonder technology became a widespread faith, so necessary as it is to maintain life and to ward off death. No wonder these architects hunger to elevate technology beyond strict utilitarianism to show how Western culture has used these tools to such dynamic effect.

Concrete, glass steel – these modern technological materials project a strong contrast to the natural surroundings.
FROM LEFT Sidley house by Edward Niles, Sonoma house by Joan Hallberg, Malibu house by Edward Niles, Sheats-Goldstein house by John Lautner.

Edward Niles
Sidley House, Malibu, California

Nothing better commemorates the Westerners' taming of the Wild West than this highly tooled object in the middle of the rugged Malibu coastal range. Yet the sleekest, most non-natural manufactured elements of this house (1990) also create bridges to the natural terrain. The taut mirrored surface in shady forecourt reflects the mountain range behind while the sliding front door frames a view of the ocean beyond. It is a jump cut, an optical collage worthy of Southern California's most popular technological industry, the movies.

The house is laid out more like a piece of machinery than a piece of architecture. The private living wing takes on the particularity of a camshaft connected to the living room by a drive train. The semicircular living room is filled with radiating steel trusses – a combination of the Eiffel Tower and the top of the Chrysler Building set like a Palladian villa in splendid isolation.

Here is all the technological faith of the early modernists, but adapted with even more exuberance and finesse than they dared. With sleekly fitted slabs of glass and finish-grade metal everywhere, this is a house that worships the details. Finally, it is a house in which the satellite dish doesn't clash with the architecture.

The shifting pattern of steel trusses and braces in the living room pavilion creates a dynamic space. Translucent walls of plastic sandwich panels insulate and allow natural light into the main living area.

ABOVE Each metal-clad pod contains a different
function in the private quarters, stretching from the
master suite's jutting deck (right) to the study, office
and exercise room (left). Because the elements were
hoisted into place by crane and plugged into the steel
spine, last-minute changes in position were possible.
Square concrete columns lift the private wing into the
air and channel the house's heating, air-conditioning
and utility lines.

RIGHT The glassy stair corridor, suspended over the
drive, connects the living areas with the private quarters.

LEFT Though mirrored surfaces mark the house
as a high-tech object, the strong symmetrical forms of
the living pavilion sit in the landscape as confidently
as a Palladian villa.

ABOVE The house is a protective wall set with its face to the
Pacific Ocean and its back to the 220-acre pine forest that
has supported the logging industry in this area for decades.
OPPOSITE Three blocks make up the residence: the guest
house, on the left, offers privacy from the main house; the
living room stands in the middle structure; the kitchen is
at right. Connecting the kitchen and the living room is the
dining room. Catwalks connect all three structures at roof
level, while clerestory windows visually separate the roof
from the house.

Joan Hallberg
Sonoma House, Stewarts Point, California

The Pacific coastline north of San Francisco is a rugged
landscape of drifting fogs. The pine-covered hills slope
gently down to jagged coves where the cold Pacific crashes
and tears against the continent. It is a place so magnificent
that one would hardly refuse to live there if the opportunity
arose – but it is also a place where chilly winds and Pacific
storms make living a challenge.

Joan Hallberg created a shelter that treads a delicate
line between exposure and safety. Built in 1992, the house is
composed of three wood-clad blocks, with more living area
added between, above and to the side to give the residents
a variety of spaces. Over the entire structure hovers a thin
galvanized-metal roof, which, with its bright silver finish,
might be mistaken for a cloud – or possibly an airplane
wing, because the house's knife-edge cuts into the wind.

Clerestory windows visually separate the roof from the
solid blocks below. The living room is a solid enclosure, like
a mead hall, with a lofty ceiling that disappears in a maze of
heavy timber trusses. The dining room, by contrast, sits
virtually outside, between two of the house's blocks, with
shelter and warmth provided by a thin tent of glass. The
kitchen settles into another of the heavy enclosed blocks,
but it pushes a glassy prow beyond the safety of the wall
and out into the elements, affording unobstructed views
of the dramatic coastline. But at the farthest point out is an
inviting fireplace, warming and providing comfort to the
people who live on this magnificent piece of earth – but
need the aid of technology to make it possible.

LEFT Beneath the roof's steel trusses, the terrace offers views like those of
a ship at sea, as well as the feeling of a promenade deck.
BELOW Every aspect of the house, from the curving roof to the treelike
structure of the interior's wood panels, reflects the dramatic setting on the
California coastline. A stair tower appears to roll up to the living room to
provide access to the roof deck. Heavy timber trusses give the living room
a secure atmosphere in stormy weather.

OPPOSITE The prowlike seating area in the kitchen offers
panoramic views up and down the wind-swept coast –
from the comfort of a chair in front of a roaring fire.
BELOW In its sunny position between two of the house's
solid blocks, the dining room conveys the festivity of an
elegant outdoor picnic table.

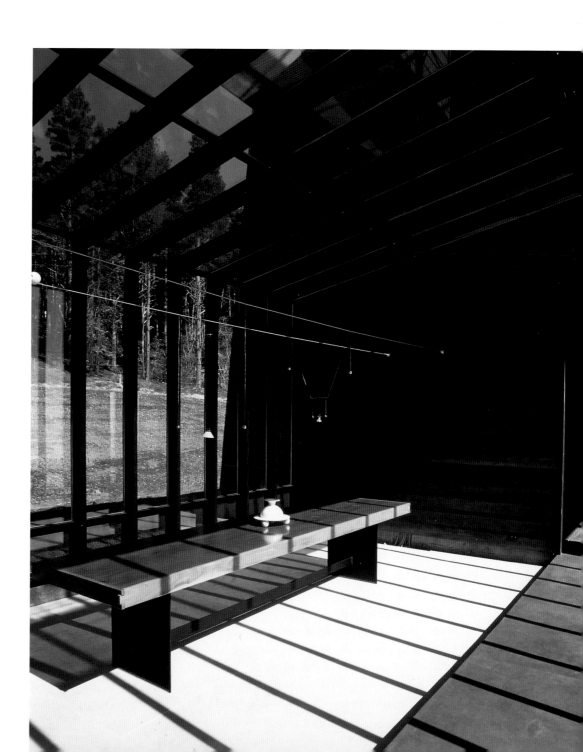

BELOW The house's muscular concrete frame is brought alive by contrasting surfaces. The architect boldly contrasts high-tech concrete with low-tech asphalt-shingle siding, and both are detailed with equal assurance and precision. The square tower contains the master shower; stairs lead to guest rooms over the garage.
OPPOSITE Sun screens on steel frames protect the living room's wraparound glass wall facing an inner courtyard. Shielded from the glaring sun on the west side and a railroad track on the east, it offers a quiet and shady alternative to the beach on the far side of the house.

Rob Wellington Quigley
Capistrano Glass House, San Clemente, California

The California beach shack is an informal shed for an informal lifestyle, with a single large room for living and dining, a sleeping loft overhead, a separate cabin for guests over the carport, low-maintenance materials inside and out, shutters and slats to cut the penetrating Western sun. This house (1993) meets all these criteria, despite a few high-tech modifications: its structure is a hefty concrete frame, complemented by steel. The greenhouse roof over the living room is a glass sandwich that reduces the heat and glare with little noticeable change in light. The bedroom loft is a sybaritic affair with a deep tub, custom fixtures and a tower shower.

In spite of its technical sophistication, the house remains a California beach shack in many appealing ways. Quigley filters the brilliant sunlight, amplified by white sand and sparkling ocean, through layers of architecture. A sitting area off the living room is shuttered with horizontal slats of wood that modulate the light of the late afternoon sun; light pouring down on the main staircase from a skylight is diffused by a strategically hung platform of wood slats. Living areas have the wide open, sunny feeling of a porch.

The asphalt shingles that face the street façade also sneak into the master bedroom, a perfect foil to the serious concrete. Indeed throughout the house, the line between inside and outside is inexact. Windows slide past walls, before angling back overhead to become roofs. This is as close as a concrete house may ever come to being light and ephemeral.

ABOVE The living room, seen from master-suite balcony, is a steel frame lean-to resting against the concrete structure. Thick concrete walls (including fireplace) set at angles enhance the carefully controlled but lively rhythms.
RIGHT Custom sinks and floating mirrors add an element of surprise to the elegant master bathroom and dressing room.
LEFT Metal stairs appear to float effortlessly from the second-floor master suite down to the living room's concrete floor. The dining room beyond looks out to the beach. Slatted screens are one element deftly used as part of the architectural vocabulary, as is the insulated plastic sandwich panel on the window, at right.

BELOW Rebuilt on the site of a house
destroyed by the 1991 Oakland hills forest
fire, the Becker house juxtaposes two similar
boxes of complementary but contrasting
materials: concrete panels on the living
room (left) and corrugated metal on the
garage (right). Decks between them provide
spacious but private outdoor areas. A glass
wall shields one deck from the street.
OPPOSITE Detail showing the precise
workmanship in fitting the concrete panels
together, the secondary grid created by
screw fasteners and the metal capping.
The house has a wood frame.

Jim Jennings

Becker House, Oakland, California

Conceived, designed, clad, detailed and built with
machine-honed precision, this residence (1994) is split
cleanly into two halves: one is a gleaming corrugated box
with a garage above and two bedrooms below, the other half
(subtly, but noticeably, bigger) contains the kitchen-living-
dining area above and the master suite below. With open-air
decks at each level connecting the two parts, corridors are
extraneous. Privacy from the street is created by a screen of
translucent glass panels. And that's the house.

Yet within this simple plan, a palette of industrial
materials creates a homage to the values of industrial
technology in the service of home. From the corrugated
aluminum siding on one wing to the concrete panels on the
other, from the glowing gray-green of slabs of glass used as
screens in the master bedroom and the entrance, these
materials are held to a narrow spectrum of grays and silvers,
black and white, composed to delicately modulate and
amplify natural light. High ceilings and clerestory light give
the main living space a grandeur that matches the panorama
framed at one end: a view of downtown Oakland, the San
Francisco skyline, the Golden Gate Bridge and the
brooding presence of Mount Tamalpais in the north.

The simply yet grandly proportioned forms of the
house match the lofty setting high on a ridge. From the
lower level a wide flight of Alaskan yellow cedar stairs,
suspended between the two wings, leads down to the
ground, and a terrace. The steps are scaled as if to be a
fragment of a much larger estate, an amphitheater for
orations to the Bay Area, but they are perfectly functional
as a place for parties, lounging and even occasional faculty
meetings held by the owner-professor.

OPPOSITE, LEFT A living-dining-kitchen space
is distinguished by tall ceilings, clerestory
windows and ebony-toned "saddlebags" –
framed boxes for storage or display recessed
between the main structural columns.
OPPOSITE, RIGHT The master bedroom's
glass partition, resting on a wood platform,
exposes luminous and austere details that are
seen everywhere. In a house of such simplicity,
these carefully balanced proportions and subtle
details are masterfully executed.
RIGHT Frosted-glass partitions rise in
continuous sheets from the master bedroom
into the living area above. A fireplace is placed
into metal veneer on the wall.

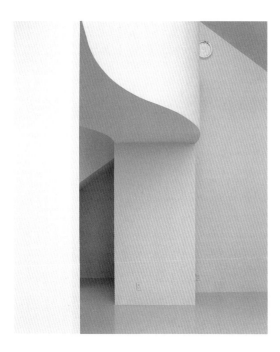

David Ireland

Ireland House, San Francisco, California

This house (1982) speaks the urban vernacular: corrugated siding, simple gables, truck doors and oversize light monitors. Yet for all the utilitarianism of these rough materials and simple structures, the building is clearly an artistic interpretation of its working-class environs, rendered in plain shades of gray. The random shapes seen along the modest block are given clarity and aesthetic order in this corner house and gallery.

The anonymous front door opens into the living room, a two-story space sliced through with an S-shaped bridge-balcony. A switchback stair ascends one of the room's wall to the bridge. A lightwell sits low on the wall on one side, while clerestories and slit windows allow in finely tuned light, balanced and continuous through the day. The simple white walls are a charming composition of shade and brightness.

Upstairs is a loft area and a bedroom that are lighted by huge light monitors that lead the eye up to the sky rather than the buildings across the street. A roof deck provides south light and a modicum of outdoor space on a tight, city site.

This is the work-a-day face of the industrial West. Not glamorous, not sleek, it nevertheless transcends the ordinary. It uses the shapes of warehouses and factories but does not transform them too much. Rather, it is a mirror, directing us back to the vernacular landscape's beauty.

TOP Simple shapes and corrugated siding mirror the area's industrial buildings, but fine proportions and carefully placed windows reveal the hand of an artist.

LEFT A curving balcony divides the two-story living space in half.
OPPOSITE The house, which is used for installations of furniture and art, provides a gallerylike backdrop.

ABOVE The entrance (at center) opens into an alcove beneath diagonal stairs leading to an s-shaped balcony and a loft lighted by one of the two south-facing light monitors visible on the exterior.

LEFT The range of light and shadow that play over the walls belies the simplicity of the white planes and curving balcony.

TOP Tile screens protect the gardens and courtyards on the inland side of the house. The structure is a concrete frame filled in with concrete block, a common vernacular construction method in Mexico.

ABOVE Open tile at the ends of the roof draw air into a roof cavity where it rises to perimeter peaks to be exhausted. The circulation of air cools the roof and maintains a comfortable temperature without air-conditioning. The roof's slope directs the occasional rain into scuppers and into gravel filled pits.

Steve Badanes

Baja House, Baja California, Mexico

A house thrown open to the outside, a house that captures the wind to cool itself, a house that takes its shape from the climate and its residents' lifestyle.

In Baja California, it is only the amiable white beaches that meet the ocean, not the aggressive cliffs of northern California. The dry scrub, white sand and blue ocean attract people to the seaside desert, where only the simplest of shelters is required. All one really needs is a permanent tent whose sides can be easily thrown open, a shade from the hot sun – in this case a shade that cools itself. The butterfly roof of the house (1989) appears to be swept up by off-shore winds; in fact it scoops air through the hollow tiles at each end, thereby cooling and insulating the living areas from the hot desert sun.

On the land side, walls of red-clay tile create screens covered in bougainvillea vines that shelter simple outdoor gardens paved with pebbles. Two breezeways cut through the house from front to back, and part of the kitchen tucks in under one of the breezeway's roof. Bedrooms can be shuttered with louvered doors – or they can be thrown open so that the entire side of the house is open to the sea.

The whitewashed concrete-block structure, the red-tile floors, the colorful glazed tiles used in the kitchen are all local materials that reflect the local vernacular architecture. The house is little more than a broad sweeping roof – but adapted in the right way it makes the most of the sun and outdoor lifestyle.

RIGHT The architect's solution to hot sun and fierce seasonal winds gave this house its distinctive shape. Two breezeways cool the living areas.

RIGHT Folding doors throw the entire front of the residence open to the northeastern view of the Sea of Cortez along Baja California's coastline.

BELOW LEFT The open floorplan connects the open breezeways and courts with the kitchen and living rooms.

Antoine Predock

Zuber House, Paradise Valley, Arizona

Another house that honors the starkness of the desert mountains and the mines, machines and train tracks that made habitation possible. From the outside the Zuber residence (1989) is square and flat roofed; two angled towers standing out from the flat face force an orderly symmetry onto the façade, but the wings that spread out from the center break the careful balance.

At the heart of the house is a pool of water, with a cascade and channels that direct it into the living areas. Surrounding this shady oasis is a four-sided tower housing the multilevel master suite. A ramp leads from the living room to the office overlooking the pool. A few steps circling the pool court lead to the vaulted master bedroom and its desert view. The sound of water can be heard through all the windows facing the court.

A red metal bridge leads out from one front tower. It is a long and unusually thin deck, more like a railroad trestle than a patio. The bridge also marks the house's entrance, with stairs passing just beneath it and winding up to the rear of the house, where the front door is in a shady outdoor room. Light in the desert can be harsh and blinding, but the house shields its occupants. On the south side windows with fixed metal screens of horizontal steel ribbons keep the sunlight out but usher the views in.

ABOVE LEFT Minimal materials and color palette characterize the house's lean aesthetic.
LEFT Towers making deep shadows and metal screens shield windows from the searing sun, allowing indirect light inside and unobstructed views of the outside.

A fortress against the heat, this residence rises out of native plants on
a desert hillside. The vaulted living room is bridged between two towers.
A trestlelike deck extends at right.

William Bruder

Hill-Sheppard House, Phoenix, Arizona

This is a tough, moody house. Built in 1992, it is located in the center of sprawling Phoenix, but it has the dusty, rustic feel of a shack in the middle of the desert nowhere. It plays with interpenetrating space and structure in the manner of R.M. Schindler, but it also has the populist feel of a recreational vehicle. In short, it is a house of contradictions – the ideal Western house.

The front gate, hidden around a corner, leads to a flight of stairs that looks and feels like a natural desert wash; irregular stone steps are lined with gutters like seeps. High, narrow concrete-block walls evoke a box canyon. The entrance court – one of three distinct outdoor areas – is a dry garden with bright yellow walls.

Entry to the house passes through a wall of glass. To the left are the tall living room and kitchen, in a trapezoidal wing. The pool terrace on one side and the backyard on the other are landscaped as pieces torn from the virgin desert; concrete-block walls with weeping mortar cancel out the neat orderliness of high-design and usher in the raw utilitarian vernacular West.

The unromanticized galvanized corrugated siding is as austere as the landscaping. The house is a real desert home – not prettified with adobe walls but tough, powerful and liberated.

ABOVE The angular laundry-room window is as much a part of the composition as every other opening in this iconoclastic home. A hanging corrugated panel detached a few inches from the wall allows light into the second-level master bath.

TOP LEFT Trapezoidal forms break the house out of the ordinary. Irregular flagstone and native plants create a spare but evocative landscape. Wide metal overhangs provide shade and add depth to the interior spaces.
RIGHT Outdoor stairs lead to the third-floor roof deck and its spectacular view of Squaw Mountain in the center of Phoenix.

BELOW Echoing the steps, the railing to the house's third floor plays on the vertical and horizontal lines that tie this detail organically to the structural system.

Wallace Cunningham

City House, La Jolla, California

A big house on a small city lot has to steal space from itself. Wallace Cunningham used glass walls, lofty ceilings and a complex fabric of interwoven spaces to make the most of each room, nook and view in this residence (1987). Three separate pavilions, with three outdoor courtyards weaving between them, occupy the site: the living room overlooking the street is the first; the kitchen, dining room and family room – with master bedroom and study above – are in the larger central pavilion; a guesthouse pavilion is at the rear of the lot.

The site is sliced into orderly rows of wall, four feet apart. It looks regimented, yet the walls are punctured and carved away to unify the fragmented space into flowing three-dimensional volumes. They cannot really be called rooms; they are too open. The second-floor master suite overlooks the kitchen to capture a view of the garden through a seventeen-foot-high window-wall, while the narrow third-floor hallway is expanded by an unexpected glimpse of the central patio far below through an open railing. Passages through long, low corridors end in a dramatic arrival at wide, open rooms with high ceilings.

Almost every room has a glimpse of one or two of the garden courts, and with glass filling the end of each slice, the rooms have the airy feel of being completely surrounded by greenery. If one stands in the right place, viewing the parallel walls on end, the structure nearly vanishes, leaving only a lush garden home.

RIGHT The residence presents a bold vertical face to the street: the surprise is how freely the space flows inside. At left is the living-room pavilion; on the right the main part of the house rises three floors to afford views of the Pacific Ocean.

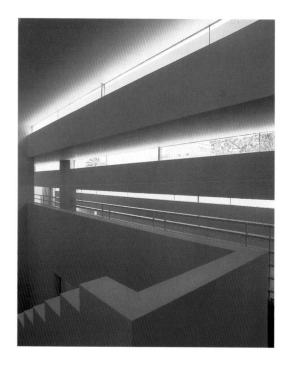

ABOVE The varying heights of the
structure's thin bays allow uninterrupted
clerestory windows to spread light
throughout the house. This balcony to the
study is on the third level.

LEFT The shaded entrance connects the
smaller living-room pavilion on the right to
the rest of the house.

OPPOSITE Glass fills the space between
the tall structural slices, which virtually
disappear – leaving the kitchen's concrete-
and-steel fixtures surrounded by light and
greenery: a house in a garden.

Steve Badanes and Jim Adamson

Hill House, Woodside, California

ABOVE On top of a 2450-foot ridge line, the house boasts views of both the Pacific Ocean and San Francisco Bay. The structure's east side is burrowed into the earth, which laps over to create the sod roof. RIGHT Lens-shaped wood and steel trusses arrayed in a sweeping arc support a roof layered over with sod and native plants. Up-ended flower pots from a discount department store serve as light fixtures.

Exploiting the warmth of the sun – an aim as old as humankind that has inspired imaginative answers around the globe. In the San Francisco Bay Area, the architects have taken the mechanics of solar technology and turned this residence (1979) into a symbiosis between the natural site and the human ecology.

Half the house is nestled into the ground, half is open to the southern sun. On the north and east sides, sloping berms insulate and protect walls that sweep up and over the roof, where a layer of soil supports a healthy meadow of native plants. The berms are carved out at the entry to form a court that shelters an outdoor garden terrace of native vegetation. Inside, the house is enlivened with rock walls, wood ceilings and hand-crafted doors. A collaborative building effort between architects and craftsmen provided the opportunity for improvisation as the house went up, and this hands-on approach to technology allowed the designers to pay special attention to the natural setting.

The panoramic living-room windows face the Pacific Ocean. Operable vents at the base of each window allow solar-heated air, which is stored below in the passive solar trombe wall (a slab of concrete oriented to the sun), to rise into the house at night.

John Lautner
    Sheats-Goldstein House, Beverly Hills, California

The Sheats-Goldstein house is a primeval cave made of twentieth-century materials. John Lautner was an artist-engineer, an unlikely combination that made him perfect for interpreting the West's conflicting love of nature and machines. When he first built this Beverly Hills hillside house for the Sheats family in 1963, he fashioned an angular roof of concrete. It starts low and intimate, nestled against the hill and rises to a cave mouth (originally sheltered only by an air screen) open to the west and the lights of Los Angeles. Glass embedded in the roof allows streaks of light to stream into the space. All the comforts of the twentieth century, but with the reassuring sheltering of one of humankind's oldest habitations.

When remodelling the house for Jim Goldstein in the 1980s, Lautner continued the autochthonous, earthy metaphor in the master bedroom on the lower level. Here the built-in concrete bed platforms, couches and tables rise like geological outcroppings from the cave floor. And to leave the view as open as possible, Lautner created a wall of glass that can slide back automatically at the touch of a button – and invented a glass sink set in a glass wall so the owner can enjoy the view while shaving.

Part of a major remodelling done twenty-five years after the house was originally built, the master bedroom juts out beneath a cantilevered pool deck on the main floor. Floor to ceiling glass cleanly encloses the master bedroom, affording an unobstructed view of Los Angeles city lights below. Glass panels that meet at the corner slide back at the push of a button, and a lounging couch and built-in concrete furniture rise out of the structure as an organic unity.

ABOVE Triangular coffers in the ceiling provide a strong
protective shelter – a high-tech cave.
OPPOSITE By day, glass embedded in the concrete roof
allows shafts of sunlight to pour into the living room.

ABOVE Clean lines devoid of trim and simple materials used in broad strokes identify the work of a master architect completely in control of massive forms and basic materials. The stairs at the end of the corridor lead from the master bedroom to the main floor above.
LEFT An outdoor passageway turns the master bedroom into a real retreat.
RIGHT The all-glass sink set in an all-glass wall is a crystalline sculpture. A chromed pipe cantilevered from the wall delivers water to the sink, which is released down the outside of the slanting glass into the floor drain when a glass stopper is removed.

BELOW Shimmering mirror glass stretched
tautly over a steel skeleton makes a bold
statement about the technology required to
live comfortably in the Southern California
desert.
OPPOSITE Curved bays modify the strict
steel grid to allow for more space in certain
areas – the residents' needs take precedence
over the dictates of the structural system.
A palette of aluminum curtain walls,
polished chrome, metal panels and glass
adds variation to the simple geometry.

Edward Niles
Malibu House, Malibu, California

A sleek mirrored box of hard edges and exact
geometry sitting on a prow of land, standing in stark
contrast to the surroundings. Weathered red stone of
fractilian geometry circles around it at a wary distance on
the horizon. Millions of years of geological upthrust and
erosion are pitted against an outpost of technological skill –
it's a standoff.

Like the standard steel-frame office buildings of
Century City and downtown Los Angeles, this house (1995)
is a steel cage. Identical frames – each an 'H' with a broken
cross bar – repeat in a straight row. Like the towers of the
Golden Gate Bridge, the vertical members create corridors
on either side along the length of the cage. A gabled
skylight of insulated fiberglass panels connects the towers
and roofs the main living space, while a glass skin wraps
around the outside of the cage, taut as shrinkwrap.

Within this regular frame, rooms are contained in
cylinders or in the spaces left over between cylinders and
partitions. Sometimes they need more space than the
frame's boundary allows, and so the skin bulges outward.
The frame is changeable, warped to the needs of the space
inside – a bay of glass in one of the children's rooms,
a garden cut around the chimney. A tight palette of gray
stone, metallic panels, polished chrome and smoked glass
clads the entire house, inside and out.

The steel, the glass, the box – these are clichés of the
corporate-industrial landscape. But with its flexibility, this
house breathes life into these features. Machined surfaces
have a meaning in this wild setting that they usually lack in
an urban context: they are a confident statement of the
human presence.

ABOVE Bedrooms retain the same metallic finishes that appear throughout the house. A canopy imparts an intimate scale.

LEFT Several architectural systems are combined in the living room. The exposed steel frame establishes corridors down both sides of the house, while its wider central section opens up for the living spaces.

ABOVE Standardized metal curtain walls and doors, used
in typical commercial storefronts, are employed for the front
door, which faces onto an entrance plaza.

LEFT A soaking tub in the dressing room overlooks the
surrounding coastal mountains.

RIGHT Metal finishes in the living areas are a constant
reminder of the machine in making life in the West possible.
This view is from the study into kitchen.

Bibliography

These books can lead the interested reader into more examples of the designs of Hyperwest architects, or into the background or inspiration for their work. Several books have more than one architect represented; when the architect's name is shown in brackets after the entry, he or she is the primary subject of the publication.

Aidala, Thomas R., *Hearst Castle/San Simeon*, Harrison House, New York, 1981.

Antoine Predock, Architect, Rizzoli, New York, 1994.

Architectural Review, April, 1996 [William Bruder].

Betsky, Aaron, John Chase and Leon Whiteson, *Experimental Architecture in Los Angeles*, Rizzoli, New York, 1991.

Boutelle, Sara Holmes, *Julia Morgan, Architect*, Abbeville Publishers, New York, 1988.

Bunting, Bainbridge, *John Gaw Meem: Southwest Architect*, University of New Mexico Press, Albuquerque, New Mexico, 1983.

Cardwell, Kenneth H., *Bernard Maybeck: Artisan, Architect, Artist*, Peregrine Smith, Inc., Salt Lake City, 1977.

Chase, John, *Exterior Decoration: Hollywood's Inside-out Houses*, Hennessey and Ingalls, Inc., Los Angeles, 1982

Cheney, Sheldon, *The New World Architecture*, Tudor Publishing Co., New York, 1935.

Crosbie, Michael J., *The Jersey Devil Design/Build Book*, Peregrine Smith Books, Salt Lake City, 1984 [Steve Badanes].

Crosbie, Michael J., *Green Architecture: A Guide to Sustainable Design*, Rockport Publishers, Rockport, Massachusetts, 1994 [Steve Badanes].

Davis, Sam, *The Architecture of Affordable Housing*, University of California Press, Berkeley, 1995 [Rob Wellington Quigley].

DeLong, David, *Bruce Goff: Toward an Absolute Architecture*, MIT Press, Cambridge, Massachusetts, 1988.

Emmerling, Mary, *American Country West*, Clarkson N. Potter Inc., New York, 1985 [Charles F. Johnson].

Engelbrecht, Lloyd C. and June-Marie, *Henry C. Trost: Architect of the Southwest*, El Paso Public Library Association, El Paso, Texas, 1981.

Escher, Frank, *John Lautner, Architect*, Artemis, London, 1994.

"Friends of Kebyar," *Architecture + Urbanism*, No. 174, March, 1985.

GA Houses and Projects, nos. 18, 28, 32, 34, 37,38, 46, 48, A.D.A. Edita, Tokyo [Edward Niles].

GA Houses no. 19, "Meet the Architect: Bart Prince," A.D.A. Edita, Tokyo, 1986.

Gebhard, David and Robert Winter, *Los Angeles: An Architectural Guide*, Gibbs-Smith Publishers, Salt Lake City, 1994.

Gebhard, David, *Schindler*, The Viking Press, New York, 1971.

Gebhard, David, *Tulsa Art Deco*, The Junior League of Tulsa, Inc., Tulsa, Oklahoma, 1980.

Gebhard, David, Eric Sandweiss and Robert Winter, *The Guide to Architecture in San Francisco and Northern California*, Gibbs M. Smith, Inc., Salt Lake City, 1985.

Jodidio, Phillip, *Contemporary American Architects*, Benedikt Taschen GMBH, Germany, 1993.

Jodidio, Phillip, *Contemporary California Architects*, Benedikt Taschen, Italy, 1995.

Larson, Magali Sarfatti, *Behind the Post-Modern Facade*, Princeton Press, Princeton, New Jersey, 1993 [Rob Wellington Quigley].

Longstreth, Richard, *On the Edge of the World: Four Architects in San Francisco at the Turn of the Century*, MIT Press, Cambridge, Massachusetts, 1983.

March, Lionel and Judith Sheine, editors, *R.M. Schindler: Composition and Construction*, Academy Editions/Ernst und Sohn, London, 1995.

Mather, Christine and Sharon Woods, *Santa Fe Style*, Rizzoli, New York, 1986 [Charles F. Johnson].

McCoy, Esther, *Case Study Houses: 1945–1962*, Hennessey and Ingalls, Inc., Los Angeles, 1977.

McCoy, Esther, *Five California Architects*, Praeger Publishing, New York, 1960.

Mead, Christopher, *Houses by Bart Prince*, University of New Mexico Press, Albuquerque, New Mexico, 1991.

Moore, Charles, Gerald Allen and Donlyn Lyndon, *The Place of Houses*, Holt Rinehart and Winston, New York, 1974.

Ojeda, Oscar Riera, editor, *The New American House*, Whitney Library of Design, New York, 1995.

Pearson, David, *The Natural House Book*, Simon & Schuster Inc., New York, 1989 [Charles F. Johnson].

Rigan, Otto, *From the Earth Up*, McGraw-Hill, New York, 1979 [James Hubbell].

Rob Wellington Quigley: Buildings + Projects, Rizzoli, New York, 1996.

Storrer, William Allin, *The Architecture of Frank Lloyd Wright: A Compleat Catalog*, MIT Press, Cambridge, Massachusetts, 1978.

Stoughton, Kathleen, curator, *Wallace E. Cunningham: Environmental Design*, Mesa College Art Gallery, San Diego, 1991.

Street-Porter, Tim, *The Los Angeles House*, Clarkson N. Potter Inc., New York, 1995.

Sutro, Dirk, *West Coast Wave*, Van Nostrand Reinhold, New York, 1994.

Woodbridge, Sally, editor, *Bay Area Houses*, Gibbs-Smith Publishers, Salt Lake City, 1988.

Woodbridge, Sally, *Maybeck: Visionary Architect*, Abbeville, New York, 1992.